Rod of Iron
KINGDOM

Hyung Jin Sean Moon

God bless!

ISBN 978-1-7324006-0-3
e-book ISBN 978-1-7324006-1-0

Published by
Rod of Iron Ministries
889 Main Street, P.O. Box 557
Newfoundland, PA 18445
www.RodofironMinistries.org

Books are available in quantity for promotional use.
For information on discounts and terms, visit our website:
www.RodofironMinistries.org

ROD OF IRON
KINGDOM

Hyung Jin Sean Moon

"An excellent apologetic for the 2nd Amendment.
A handbook for dealing with some of the big mistakes people make
when talking about the 2nd Amendment, self-defense and limiting the
power of government. I would urge people to get a copy!"

Larry Pratt, Executive Director Emeritus
Gun Owners of America

"Pastor Sean's new book sounds the alarm for 2nd Amendment
supporters! The very first page starts you off with explosive new
evidence detailing WHY our government will always fail to protect its
citizens. Pastor Sean details embarrassing and illogical public policy
- all while presenting a call to action for Christian believers to unite
and take action. This book outlines in perfect clarity the real reasons
people need to follow my motto to: Get armed. Get trained. Carry
daily. A must read!"

Andrew Hallinan,
Florida Gun Supply

"Pastor Hyung Jin Moon provides a complete historical argument
for the absolute need to protect and defend the Second Amendment.
"Rod of Iron Kingdom" is the fully loaded magazine that every
patriot needs going into a war of words with any liberal gun
grabber."

Pastor George C. Cook,
Nehemiah Center for Worship

Acknowledgements

This book is drawn from 16 sermons that I've given over the last year based on the theme, "Kingdom of the Rod of Iron."

I'd like to acknowledge the efforts of Richard Panzer and Kerry Williams, the two lead researchers, as well as Regis Hanna and Robert Morton who reviewed the manuscript. Thanks also to Rod Cameron, for all of his efforts on the cover design, and to PierAngelo Beltrami, for his work on the layout.

I'd also like to acknowledge the writings of author/filmmaker Dinesh D'Souza in exposing the threat to the American republic posed by leftwing fascism, the fact-finding of the Crime Prevention Research Center and reports from the American Civil Rights Union concerning the racist origins of gun control laws. I also want to express my indebtedness to the important work of the National Rifle Association and Gun Owners of America in defending our 2nd Amendment rights.

Most of all I'd like to express my gratitude to my father, Rev. Sun Myung Moon, for his absolute faith and commitment to carry on Jesus' work to establish God's Kingdom on earth, and also to my older brother Kook Jin Justin Moon who encouraged me to stand up in the anointing given to me by my father.

Table of Contents

Introduction / 9

Chapter 1
Parkland, Florida / 13

Chapter 2
Newfoundland, Pennsylvania / 19

Chapter 3
Civil War in the Western World / 27

Chapter 4
Leftwing Fascist Threat to Democracy / 35

Chapter 5
The Challenge of Political Islam / 43

Chapter 6
Our Judeo-Christian Foundation Protects Freedom for All / 57

Chapter 7
He Shall Rule Them with a Rod of Iron / 67

Chapter 8
Legal Firearm Use Saves Lives / 79

Chapter 9
Racist Origins of Gun Control / 91

Chapter 10
Peace Police Peace Militia / 99

Chapter 11
The Choice / 109

Endnotes / 121

.

Introduction

*In February 2018, our small church in the sleepy town of
Newfoundland, Pennsylvania held a Marriage Blessing
ceremony and invited members from around the world to
bring their AR-15 rifles. Planning this event had begun more
than six months before. Although there was concern about the
recent tragic events in the Parkland, Florida school shooting,
it was our sense that if God had inspired us six months ago, He
wasn't going to change His mind due to one lunatic. There was
no way we could have anticipated the firestorm of publicity
that followed. "Gun Church in PA Blesses AR-15's!" and "The
Gun Church in Pennsylvania!" screamed the headlines. This
book tells the real reasons for the ceremony, and how they are
related to the serious challenges facing our nation and world.*

****

*My parents named me Hyung Jin and I took the English
name "Sean" because growing up in America it was easier
for people to remember. My father, the Reverend Sun Myung
Moon, raised me and my 12 siblings in Irvington, New York, a
small town in Westchester County about 45 minutes north of
New York City. We lived on a 19 acre church compound and if
we were not married we were not allowed to leave the property
without permission and security. Our family received many*

death threats over the years, and so we were not permitted to wander the neighborhoods, hang out with friends or ride our bikes outside the gates. To us, it seemed like a prison, but in retrospect I believe our parents were simply doing their best to try and keep us safe.

Being cloistered on that property, my siblings and I found avenues to cope with our secluded lives. Some got into art or music, while others worked on cars and bikes. I was drawn to learn about martial arts. I fell in love with the idea of self-defense after being bullied when I was young. Martial arts became my youthful obsession. I would spend 7-9 hours a day studying, exercising and practicing in dojos in order to become "bullyproof."

As I grew older, my passion for self-defense began to include weapons arts such as the katana, bow staff, and meteor hammer. Eventually I began studying the use of firearms, or the "Way of the Rod of Iron."

Before he passed on, my father strongly encouraged me to pursue excellence in mixed martial arts, Brazilian Jiu-Jitsu and weapons arts. He loved to have me give demonstrations around the world for our congregations.

My passion for sharing the arts of self-defense is central to my family's lifestyle as well as to my Church ministry—Rod of Iron Ministries. I train with my wife, children, and members of my congregation. The knowledge of self-defense is not the study of one specific weapon; it is the study of the use of force. It is my belief that all good, law-abiding people should know how to properly utilize force in order to protect themselves against real evil. The AR-15 is a force multiplier and a tremendous tool for self, home, and property defense. It is truly a blessing that law-

abiding citizens in America can own this tool of great power which we can use to defend ourselves. The church shooting in Sutherland County, Texas, was stopped by a citizen with an AR-15, thus preventing further innocent bloodshed.

We need to be asking ourselves: "Will innocent people continue to have the right to defend themselves? Will conscientious citizens be able to utilize force equal to the force wielded by violent lawbreakers?" These are the real questions. Because God gave us free will, we can never get rid of the potential for evil. Thanks to the 2nd Amendment, we have the freedom to protect ourselves and our loved ones against the forces of evil with even greater force.

.

1
Parkland, Florida

On Valentine's Day, February 14, 2018, a mentally deranged young person named Nikolas Cruz stepped out of an Uber at the Marjory Stoneman Douglas High School in Parkland, Florida.[1]

*It was **2:19 p.m**. Two minutes later, Cruz, a former student at Stoneman Douglas, entered Building 12, carrying a duffel bag and a backpack. He began firing within a few seconds.*

Broward County Deputy Sheriff Scott Peterson, on campus at the time, was near the administration building.

*At **2:22 p.m**. the fire alarm was triggered, blaring throughout the entire campus. The first 911 call also went out, via Coral Springs emergency dispatch center.*

*"Be advised we have possible, could be firecrackers. I think we have shots fired, possible shots fired —1200 building," Peterson radioed at **2:23 p.m**.*

At that moment, Peterson arrived at the southeast corner of Building 12. "We're talking about the 1200 building, it's going to be the building off Holmberg Road," Peterson said frantically seconds later.

As the shooting progressed, first in the hallways, and then in five classrooms on the first and second floor, calls began "blowing up" the 911 call centers. Students were spilling out of the campus. Peterson radioed to make sure "no one comes inside the school." Although he could hear shots being fired inside the building, he remained outside.

At 2:27 p.m., *six minutes after Cruz went into Building 12, the shooting stopped. Cruz ditched his AR-15, vest and some ammunition in the third-floor stairwell and left.*

At 2:32 p.m. — *11 minutes after the shooting began — four Coral Springs officers and two Broward Security Officer deputies made the first police entrance into the building, helping to "extract a victim."*

Down the street, Cruz had entered a Walmart and bought a drink at the Subway inside.

At 3:40 p.m., *a Coconut Creek officer saw Cruz and arrested him without incident. Cruz was indicted the next day on 17 counts of first-degree murder and 17 counts of attempted murder. The victims included:*[2]

> *Scott Beigel, a geography teacher, who was killed as he tried to usher students back into his classroom when the shooting started.*
>
> *Aaron Feis, an assistant football coach, who was killed when he threw himself in front of students to protect them from oncoming bullets.*
>
> *Chris Hixon, the school's athletic director.*
>
> *Alyssa Alhadeff, 14*
>
> *Martin Anguiano, 14*
>
> *Nicholas Dworet, 17*
>
> *Jaime Guttenberg, 14*
>
> *Luke Hoyer, 15*
>
> *Cara Loughran, 14*
>
> *Gina Montalto, 14*
>
> *Joaquin Oliver, 17*
>
> *Alaina Petty, 14*

Meadow Pollack, 18

Helena Ramsay, 17

Alex Schachter, 14

Carmen Schentrup, 16

Peter Wang, 15

Grieving students and parents asked, "How could this have happened?" especially when there was an armed police officer on campus. Others focused on the weapon used, the AR-15 semi-automatic rifle, and called for banning the sale of such guns in the United States.

Parkland school shooting survivors appeared at a CNN townhall and on other TV news channels to demand immediate passage of legislation to limit or ban AR-15 sales. They accused legislators committed to the 2nd Amendment of being in the pocket of the National Rifle Association. Actor George Clooney and his wife gave $500,000 to a nationwide protest against gun violence.[3] Their announcement inspired similar gifts from other well-known celebrities. A recurring theme was: "the NRA has blood on its hands."

Other Parkland school shooting survivors who doubted that such laws would have prevented this or other school shootings complained that they were not allowed to speak at the CNN townhall, or that their intended comments were rejected by CNN staff.

Government's Failure to Protect Lives

This shooting tragically demonstrates the incapacity of the

government to protect its citizens. For whatever reason, Broward County Deputy Sheriff Scott Peterson failed to enter the school, to engage and stop the shooter. Other armed officers arrived too late to stop the shooting.

Before this incident, local authorities had been called *39 times* about Nikolas Cruz' erratic and violent behavior. He reportedly had dreams "of killing people and being covered in blood."[4] He was known to torture animals, had brought a backpack containing bullets to class, and made threats of violence. Law enforcement officers were alerted numerous times that Cruz might be dangerous, but chose not to take action.

The FBI failed to respond to two tips about Cruz, one of which involved Cruz posting online that he planned to become a "professional school shooter." The Broward Sheriff's Office was also warned about the teen, and had received a report that he "planned to shoot up the school."[5] Making violent threats is a felony offense that would have justified his arrest and prevented him from purchasing a firearm.

Why was he never arrested after making such threats? The answer may surprise you. Five years earlier Broward County Public Schools embraced an Obama administration policy dedicated to preventing the arrest of troubled students. In 2013, the Broward County schools rewrote their disciplinary policies to make it nearly impossible to suspend, expel, or arrest students for behavioral problems including drug use, assault, or other criminal activity. The reason? To reduce the number of minority students ending up in jail for crimes committed on campus.[6]

A leading advocate for the new disciplinary policies detailing

13 non-reportable crimes was Broward County Sheriff Scott Israel, who has shied away from responsibility for the school shooting and sought instead to blame the National Rifle Association.

Within a few years after implementing this new policy, ethnically diverse Broward went from leading Florida in student in-school arrests to having one of its lowest school-related incarceration rates. School suspensions and expulsions also dropped sharply. For students who break the law, the PROMISE (Preventing Recidivism through Opportunities Mentoring, Interventions, Support & Education) program, replaces criminal detention with counseling.[7]

The Obama administration praised Broward County's reforms. In 2015 the district's superintendent attended an event at the White House, "Rethink Discipline," that highlighted Broward's success in "transforming policies and school climate."[8]

Nikolas Cruz had been suspended from Stoneman Douglas High School. He had even been expelled for bringing firearms to school, but without an arrest record, Cruz could still buy weapons.

Despite carrying out a series of arrestable offenses on campus before the Parkland school shooting, Nikolas Cruz escaped the attention of the police, passed a background check and purchased the firearm he used to murder three staff members and 14 fellow students. All of this happened because of the implementation of Obama Education Department directives.

Cruz's school district was in the forefront of a strategy adopted by dozens of other major school districts around the country that allowed psychologically disturbed, often uncontrollable students to commit crimes without any legal consequences. The aim was to slow the "school-to-prison pipeline."[9]

Applications for federal grants reveal that Broward County School Superintendent Runcie's plan was a factor in the approval of tens of millions of dollars in federal funding from Obama Education Secretary Arne Duncan's department.[10]

This is a textbook case not only of government's inability to protect its citizens, but also of how "progressive" federal policies can override common sense at the local level.

Local school administrators and law enforcement officers were very aware that this boy was a ticking time bomb, but were prevented from taking action because the county school superintendent and the county sheriff had entered into agreements to increase federal funding. Their solution to reducing school-related crime? Don't report it.

And if anything bad happens involving the use of guns? Just blame it on the NRA.

2
Newfoundland, Pennsylvania

Newfoundland, Pennsylvania is a small, quiet town. Our religious community purchased the vacant church on Main Street a few years ago. Based on the teachings of Jesus and my father, Rev. Sun Myung Moon, we have held weekly Sunday worship services and a number of Holy Marriage Blessings involving members from here and around the world, without any press attention or controversy.

That suddenly changed after the Parkland shooting. An event we planned many months earlier suddenly became front-page news. More than 40 journalists from over two dozen news organizations came to record our February 28 "Book of Life" Blessing event. Newspapers and TV broadcasts, reaching more than a billion people from almost every continent in the world, informed their viewers and readers with lurid headlines of an "AR-15 Blessing."

Pennsylvania Church to Hold
Controversial Blessing of AR-15s

With A Rod Of Iron: AR-15-Toting So-Called Churchgoers Renew Their Commitment To the Blood-Soaked Lunacy of Our Nation Amen

by Abby Zimet, staff writer

WEIRD NEWS

Pennsylvania Church Holds Marriage Ceremony with Guns

Couples clutch AR-15 rifles as they renew wedding vows

Mar 1, 2018   (2)

Church blesses AR-15-wielding couples wearing crowns made of bullets and says guns would have stopped Florida shooting

The World Peace and Unification Sanctuary promises global unity through heavy firepower

It's 2018 and People Are Wearing Bullet Crowns and Praying with Their AR-15s

Everything is fine.

Here are just some of the more "restrained" emails we received:

You and your church are complicit in the deaths of the 17 school children and teachers who died at the Parkland school in Florida. You are complicit in the deaths of all who died in the Nevada concert mass shooting. You are complicit in the deaths of all who died in the Orlando night club shooting. You are complicit. When you condone the ownership, use and abuse of war weapons by non-military people, you are complicit in the deaths of innocent Americans. Catherine S.

It's people like all of you that are the reason that religion is dying right now. You are laughable and I hope that your kind die out soon. Maybe some crazies in your congregation can use their assault rifles on the other crazies and solve the problem for the SANE Americans that don't want all of you here. You are all disturbed and despicable. Shame on all of you. Adam C.

As a Christian I can tell you that ALL your souls are damned to eternal Hell. What a pathetically sick group of people you are. I pray for you. May God help you. Russ M.

*Guess you can justify anything...if you're warped. So I guess Jesus is all for any size slaughter machine you want? Sick and compromising f***s that you are. KD*

Unconscionable amazing stupidity! RTB

Well, you get the idea. Press reports and angry emails aside, we were not "blessing guns." On February 28, several hundred couples from around the world gathered to dedicate their marriages to each other and most importantly to God.

We do not worship guns, or as we describe it, the "rod of iron." We worship God who created us in His image and desires to have a personal relationship with each one of us. We seek His blessing on our marriages because we believe that He dwells most deeply in the love between husband and wife, and between parents and children. Such blessed marriages are the building blocks of strong communities and the Kingdom of Heaven on earth.

God's desire for the human race is expressed in His words to the first human ancestors as recorded in Genesis 1:28:

And God blessed them, and God said unto them, Be fruitful, and multiply, and replenish the earth, and subdue it: and have dominion over the fish of the sea, and over the fowl of the air, and over every living thing that moveth upon the earth.

For us, the first Blessing, "be fruitful," means to become spiritually mature. The second Blessing, "multiply," means to establish a marriage and family that is centered on God. The third Blessing, "have dominion," means that all humanity has the right to establish a godly sovereignty, based on His principles and character.

Unfortunately, our first ancestors were not able to fulfill the "Three Blessings" due to the sin of the Fall. Their fall involved the gaining of self-centered carnal "knowledge." God's ideal for individual spiritual maturity, blessed marriages, and godly dominion over the earth was never established. For members of Unification Sanctuary, the Holy Blessing ceremony is not just a marriage. It is the engrafting of one's marriage and family into the unfallen royal lineage of Christ, referred to in Revelation 19:9 as the "Marriage Supper of the Lamb."

In the Book of Revelation, Christ speaks repeatedly of "ruling with a rod of iron" (Revelation 2:27), but "ruling" is translated from the Greek word *poimaino*, which means to "shepherd" or "guard." Therefore the scripture tells us that God will protect His children with the rod of iron, guarding the flock not as a dictator, but as a loving father.

In the same way, each of us is called to use the power of the "rod of iron" not to harm or oppress (as has been done in the satanic kingdoms of this world), but to protect God's Kingdom and its inhabitants.

You and I are responsible to protect our families, communities and, ultimately, our nation. The "rod of iron" gives men, women and the elderly the ability to protect themselves and others from predators. If the football coach who rushed into the school building to defend students from the shooter with his own body had been allowed to carry a firearm, many lives, including his own, could have been saved.

Police officers are not really the "first responders" in most life and death situations. You and I are. In a crisis, it may take 10-20 minutes, sometimes much longer, for police to arrive, determine what is happening, who is involved and what, if anything, can be done about it. In the case of the Parkland shooting, most of the officers arrived too late to stop it. All they could do was help the wounded, carry out the dead bodies, and write the crime report.

True faith in God is not a fairy tale world of delusion. It involves men and women taking responsibility to love God and their neighbor, willing to defend others at the risk of their own lives. That is what my father taught me before he passed on, and what I teach and practice with my own children and the Sanctuary Church community.

My father, who was born in what is now North Korea, understood what happens when people are defenseless. When the Communists took over, he was arrested for preaching a Christian message, and sent to Hungnam death camp where people were routinely starved and worked to death. He survived because a military force led by General Douglas MacArthur liberated him and the other prisoners. Many members of his own family and countless others died.

My father forgave the men who tortured him and killed his relatives, even meeting with dictator Kim Il Sung to offer help to bring North Korea into the modern age. He also started a firearms company in South Korea after the war because he didn't want his nation and its people to ever be defenseless again.

God wishes for us to be his co-heirs and co-inheritors of the earth in the Kingdom (see Romans 8, Psalm 2). That is why I asked couples attending the February 28 Blessing ceremony to bring their "rod of iron." The purpose of the Rod of Iron is not to harm others, but to defend innocent life. As my father said, "Without a protected domain, life is threatened, and when life is threatened, love cannot manifest itself."

3
Civil War in the Western World

America is a deeply divided nation. We see dramatic evidence of this every four years in the ordeal that we call the presidential elections, involving voter battles between "blue states" and "red states."

However, this division is more than a political debate about the role of government and its policies. It is essentially a debate between those who accept and affirm the existence and authority of a Supreme Being, i.e. God, versus a belief in the "enlightened" class of "experts" who view such beliefs of God as immaturity rooted in ignorance.

18th century German philosopher Immanuel Kant expressed it this way:

Enlightenment is man's emergence from his self-incurred immaturity. Immaturity is the inability to use one's own understanding without the guidance of another.[1]

Ever since the Enlightenment, many came to see the universe as a place governed by physical laws and not by "divine providence." With the advancements of science, they thought humanity no longer needed God as the source of moral values or order in the universe. Reason itself and science were sufficient.

Many were glad to be rid of such obligations. Friedrich Nietzsche wrote:

Indeed, at hearing the news that 'the old god is dead,' we philosophers and 'free spirits' feel illuminated by a new dawn.[2]

Even though Nietzsche rejoiced at this liberation, he also foresaw a dark underside:

When one gives up the Christian faith, one pulls the right to Christian morality out from under one's feet. This morality is by no means self-evident... Christianity is a system, a whole view of things thought out together. By breaking one main concept out of it, the faith in God, one breaks the whole.[3]

In other words, without faith in a sovereign God, there really is no philosophical basis to maintain Christian values or morality. Murder is wrong? Who says so? You might think it's always wrong, but others may view it differently. Is stealing wrong? There may be laws against both, but what if the laws change? Should morality just be based on what the law requires? What happens when there is a disparity between the law and people's actual values and behavior?

Although personally an atheist, Nietzsche foresaw a difficult and even catastrophic future for a post-Christian Europe:

What I relate is the history of the next two centuries. I describe what is coming, what can no longer come differently: the advent of nihilism...For some time now our whole European culture has been moving as toward a catastrophe.[4]

When God is "Dead," you believe in such things as:

- **Nihilism-** The belief that life has no intrinsic meaning or value.

- **Materialism**- All things, including thoughts, choices and consciousness, are the results of material interactions only.

- **Eugenics**- Since there is no inherent value to human life and since evolution creates dominant species, some races are "superior" to others. Thus, actions to reduce the population of "inferior" sub-species/races and increase the population of "superior" races are legitimate.

Nietzsche foresaw that when people have concluded that God is dead, they are likely to worship secular causes or institutions, such as **National Socialism**- a State that worships and defends the interests of your race, even using power or violence against other races. Or **Communism**- a Marxist dictatorship that exploits the interests of the "working class" and seeks validation by appeals to "class hatred" and "class-warfare."

The 20th Century provided ample evidence of what can happen when people replace faith in God with a secular ideology. The racial identity ideology adopted by the German National Socialist Workers Party, which took power in the 1930s, led to the deaths of 13-21 million human beings. Communist ideology led to the deaths of an estimated 150 million civilians in the 20th century alone. Government-sponsored mass killings or "democide" led to the deaths of 6 times more people, 262 million in all, than died in combat during all the foreign and internal wars of the last century.[5]

Needless to say, when speaking of the desire of government to remove unwanted members of the population, it does not help if citizens are armed. There is a chilling pattern of gun confiscation and registration directly preceding outbreaks of mass murder, i.e. genocide. Examples include:[6]

- The Turkish government tightened gun control in advance of the Armenian genocide that began in 1915.

- Germany banned firearm sales to Jews in 1938. From 1939 to 1945 a total of 13 million[7] unarmed and disarmed Jews and other ethnic groups were sent to concentration camps and exterminated.

- The Soviet Union instituted gun control in 1929, confiscating weapons from a Soviet population that had always been heavily armed. From 1929 to 1953, about 20 million dissidents, now lacking any means for self-defense, were herded together and slaughtered.

- China's gun control program was launched by the Republic of China in 1938. From 1948 to 1952, 20 million political dissidents with no means of self-defense were massacred by the Communist government. An additional 53 million were killed through government policies that caused mass starvation.

- Cambodia instituted gun control laws in 1956. From 1975 to 1977, over one million people who were considered to have been "contaminated" by education or contact with Western values or culture were eliminated.

- Guatemala implemented gun control regulations in 1964, in advance of killing 100,000 Mayan Indians.

- Uganda launched its gun control program in 1970, just before an eight-year reign of terror resulted in thousands of Christians being put to death.

Such horrors were deeply rooted in post-Christian ideologies and political movements which dehumanized members of different racial, religious or class groups. These ideologies viewed the state as the proper agent to eliminate the demonized. Mainstream media was complicit with government-engineered mass murder. Journalists who already agreed with a national ideology or cause found a multitude of ways to portray their actions in a positive light.

One infamous example was New York Times correspondent Walter Duranty, who received the prestigious Pulitzer Prize in 1932 for his series of articles praising the "progressive" Communist leaders of the Soviet Union. His articles deceived New York Times readers about the forced starvation of nearly 4 million Ukrainian farmers.[8]

Unfortunately, such dishonest coverage of totalitarian causes and governments is widespread. A current example is the massive suffering and deaths resulting from widespread starvation and malnutrition taking place in the formerly prosperous nation of Venezuela.

While the democratic opposition petitioned for audits of voter rolls, Socialist president Hugo Chavez built secret networks with the help of the Iranian and Syrian governments as well as the Hezbollah terrorist organization. He also brought in the Cuban secret police to spy on Venezuelans.[9]

The dictatorship of Chavez's successor, Nicolas Maduro, was supported by Cuba, Iran, Russia and Syria. It has taken steps to eliminate the democratic opposition that includes providing food only to supporters of the Communist regime. Hyperinflation and price controls have led to critical shortages. Basic medical supplies are nowhere to be found on store shelves. People are dying of treatable diseases.[10]

Fascists dehumanize racial groups they don't like. Communists, who claim to be "Anti-Fascists," vilify "enemies of the working class," i.e. anyone who won't cooperate with their agenda. What both ideologies ignore is that the human capacity for extreme good or evil exists among all races and classes. Worshipping your own identity group, class or race is an ungodly worldview that has a bloody track record any moral person would want to avoid.

Meanwhile, a report released in early 2018 warns that "Christians now face worse persecution than at any time in history." *Persecuted and Forgotten* warns that

Christians in many countries will not survive if violence against them continues. The report highlighted "unspeakable atrocities" around the world including in North Korea where believers face "enforced starvation, abortion, and reports of faithful being hung on crosses over a fire and others being crushed under a steamroller."

The report adds:

Not only are Christians more persecuted than any other faith group, but ever-increasing numbers are experiencing the very worst forms of persecution. As well as persecution in the Middle East at the hands of Islamic extremism, the report also outlines abuses in Nigeria where the Islamist ISIS-affiliate Boko Haram has displaced nearly 2 million people.

...The pervasive nature of persecution – and evidence implicating regimes with whom the West has close trading and strategic links – means that it behooves our governments to use their influence to stand up for minorities, especially Christians. No longer should Christians be sacrificed on the altar of

strategic expediency and economic advantage.

Meanwhile, most people in America have heard little or nothing about such ongoing atrocities and loss of freedom, especially of Christians and other religious minorities. On college campuses, rather than opposing mass murders of Christians and other minority faiths, many students fight any "micro-aggression" that make them feel uncomfortable.

When people lose sight of the existence of real good and evil, they will dream up first world "micro" fantasy causes to fight. This is good news for the totalitarians whose relentless march aims to eliminate Judeo-Christian thought as well as Jews and Christians around the world.

4
The Leftwing Fascist Threat to the West

By the mid 20th century, with the Communist body count rising into the tens of millions, the Marxist critique of capitalism was in need of a public relations offensive. With the willing help of the mainstream media, Leftists were able to focus public attention on the recent genocide in Nazi Germany, while minimizing the staggering and ever-increasing death toll of other groups in the Soviet Union, China, Vietnam, Cambodia, and Cuba.

Anyone who openly questioned Leftist support for Communist dictatorships or socialism was quickly labeled a "Nazi." As pointed out by Anthony Gregor, a scholar of Italian fascism, the "fascism" label is routinely applied to anyone who is a professed Christian, advocates lower taxes, less government regulation, expresses skepticism about man-made "global warming," or who seems unconcerned about the decline in "endangered species."[1] Ironically, real fascists advocated none of these positions.

The term "Nazi" refers to members of the "National Socialist Workers Party." Nazis were socialists with a nationalistic agenda and a bias towards the Aryan race. They wanted more government control and regulation of people's lives, not less.

Believe it or not, New Deal Democrat President Franklin
Delano Roosevelt admired Mussolini and his fascist agenda
for its centralized government planning and action. On May 7,
1933, just a few months after Roosevelt's inauguration, *New
York Times* reporter Anne O'Hare McCormick wrote that the
atmosphere in Washington was "strangely reminiscent of Rome
in the first weeks after the march of the Blackshirts, [and] of
Moscow at the beginning of the Five-Year Plan... America
today literally asks for orders." The Roosevelt administration,
she added, "envisages a federation of industry, labor and
government after the fashion of the corporative State as it
exists in Italy."[2]

Throughout the 1930s, intellectuals and journalists noted "areas
of convergence among the New Deal, Fascism, and National
Socialism." All three were seen as transcending "classic
Anglo-French liberalism" of individualism, free markets, and
decentralized power.[3]

As described by Wolfgang Schivelbusch, in his book *Three
New Deals: Reflections on Roosevelt's America, Mussolini's
Italy, and Hitler's Germany, 1933 – 1939,* "American
Progressives studied at German universities" and "came to
appreciate the Hegelian theory of a strong state and Prussian
militarism as the most efficient way of organizing modern
societies that could no longer be ruled by anarchic liberal
principles."[4]

Roosevelt himself called Mussolini "admirable" and professed
that he was "deeply impressed by what he has accomplished."
Mussolini reciprocated the admiration. In a laudatory review
of Roosevelt's 1933 book *Looking Forward*, Mussolini wrote,
"Reminiscent of Fascism is [Roosevelt's] principle that the
state no longer leaves the economy to its own devices...

Without question, the mood accompanying this sea change resembles that of Fascism."[5]

The chief Nazi newspaper, *Volkischer Beobachter*, repeatedly praised "Roosevelt's adoption of National Socialist strains of thought in his economic and social policies" and "the development toward an authoritarian state" based on the "demand that collective good be put before individual self-interest."[6]

In 1944, in *The Road to Serfdom*, the economist F.A. Hayek warned that economic planning could lead to totalitarianism. He cautioned Americans and Britons not to think that there was something uniquely evil about the German soul. National Socialism, he said, drew on collectivist ideas that had permeated the Western world for a generation or more.[7]

Although many of their presidential policies sought to limit the power of the state, Ronald Reagan was, and now Donald Trump is, regularly accused in mainstream news media of being a new "Hitler" or "Nazi." Why debate policy issues when you can much more easily demonize your political opponent as an uncaring "fascist"?

E Pluribus Unum?

The founding vision of America is expressed in the national motto, "e pluribus unum," meaning "out of many, one." No matter what race, faith or nationality, all are welcomed to participate in the American dream with its guarantees of "unalienable rights to life, liberty and the pursuit of happiness." In Martin Luther King's famous words, people would be "judged by the content of their character," not by the color of their skin.

But with their focus on "diversity," Leftists turn the national motto upside down to "out of one, many." According to their post-modern "multicultural" narrative, the founding ideals are really just a cover for "white, male privilege." In their view, we are NOT one. We are a "diverse" collection of races and an ever-expanding collection of racial/ gender/ transgender/ LGBTQ groups which seek to use government power to impose "equality," and redistribute wealth from those who allegedly stole it to those who, as past victims, deserve it.

A widely spoken trope on college campuses across the nation is the story of "white privilege." A Texas State University campus newspaper editorial, "Your [white] DNA is an abomination," explains that "whiteness in the United States" is a "construct used to perpetuate a system of racist power," and that:

White death will mean liberation for all...Until then, remember this: I hate you because you shouldn't exist. You are both the dominant apparatus on the planet and the void in which all other cultures, upon meeting you, die.[8]

But if America is such a horrible bastion of white supremacy, then why do so many Africans, Asians, and Latin Americans want to come to the U.S., even risking their lives to get here? How is it that first generation immigrants from these parts of the world fare better than the average American who has lived here for many generations? Maybe they understand something about America that most university students in the U.S. don't -- that in America hard work can lead to opportunities undreamed of in their homelands.

Surely, there are privileges for a majority population in any country, whether you're talking about Japanese in Japan, Chinese in China, or those of European ancestry in the U.S. However, how do advocates of identity politics explain why a "minority group," Asians, living in the U.S. have the highest median income of any ethnic group, $81,000, 33% higher than "whites?"[9]

I would think long and hard before sending my children to study at most universities where they will be indoctrinated to despise the nation God has blessed to be the most free and prosperous country in the world.

ANTIFA

At "antifascist" rallies held across the nation, groups like ANTIFA whose members dress in black, their faces covered by scarves emblazoned with a Communist hammer and sickle, march with banners calling upon Americans to "SMASH WHITE SUPREMACY."

The term "antifa" is often understood to be an abbreviation of "anti-fascist" or "anti-fascist action." But "antifa" actually originates from *Antifaschistische Aktion,* a German communist movement that was active in the 1930's. In the center of the photo below is an ANTIFA demonstrator wearing a cape with the hammer and sickle, the symbol for Communism.

As pointed out by author/filmmaker Dinesh D'Souza,

...the close relationship between self-styled antifascism and fascism can be seen in some little-known aspects of one of Antifa's main financial sponsors, George Soros.

The Hungarian-born Soros became a billionaire through shrewd global investments and currency manipulation; his Quantum Fund is one of the world's first private hedge funds. Soros is the main funder of some 200 leftist groups, including Planned Parenthood, MoveOn. org, and Black Lives Matter.

Soros also backs self-proclaimed antifascist groups—this year the Soros-backed group Alliance for Global Justice gave $50,000 to the militant thugs associated with the group Refuse Fascism.

Soros doesn't merely fund activism; he also funds disruptive violence. Essentially his costumed baton-wielding squadrons amount to a private army: he has created a militia of paid thugs similar to the Italian Blackshirts and the Nazi Brownshirts. Soros' strategy is to launch dozens, even hundreds, of groups and then see which ones deliver the goods. Borrowing from the field of venture capitalism, my term for what Soros does is venture thuggery, operating through paid protesters.[10]

D'Souza points to a revealing 1998 CBS Sixty Minutes interview with Soros, where he expresses no guilt for having assisted in the confiscation of Jewish property and possessions when he was a teenager in Hungary, and concludes, "Soros and the left's self-styled antifascism is a fraud because there are no fascists they are fighting. The only fascism that is recognizable in their actions is their own."[11]

The media has been a willing accomplice in the Leftist narrative to obscure its own fascist tendencies. Youtube recently shut down our Sanctuary Youtube channel, as were others listed on the Southern Poverty Law Center's "hate watch list." These included such public figures as former Presidential candidate and HUD secretary Ben Carson and Ayaan Hirsi Ali, the Somali-born feminist who speaks out for women's rights in the Islamic world and opposes forced marriage, honor violence, child marriage and female genital mutilation.

Also listed on the SPLC's "hate watch" list are the Family Research Council, the Ruth Institute, Alliance Defending

Freedom and other groups that support natural marriage and the freedom of faith guaranteed in the U.S. Bill of Rights. SPLC maliciously groups them with real racist groups like the Ku Klux Klan, which at its founding had deep ties to the Democratic Party in the South.

Karl Zinsmeister, author and Vice President of the Philanthropy Roundtable explains:

Shutting down people you don't agree with is as un-American as you can get. Rigorous debate, honest discussion, open exchange of ideas, that's the American way, but free thinking and speech are threatened by a group with a sweet sounding name, that conceals a nefarious purpose. This group is called the Southern Poverty Law Center or SPLC.[12]

Zinnmeister points out that Mark Potok, a leader of the SPLC, was videotaped saying to supporters:

...the press will describe us as 'monitoring hate groups'... I want to say plainly that our aim in life is to destroy these groups, to completely destroy them.[13]

The masterminds behind the SPLC are not eliminating hate, they are fueling it.

Because of such "McCarthyite" tactics, the SPLC itself should be seen as one of the biggest Leftwing hate groups on the planet. It is funded by George Soros and other well-off Leftists who despise Judeo-Christian values. Google/Youtube/Facebook/Twitter's alignment with the SPLC's attacks on conservative groups who adhere to America's founders' vision for limited government should send a cold chill down the back of anyone who cares about freedom.

5
The Challenge of Political Islam

While my father was alive, he hosted dozens of international conferences where leaders of different faith traditions were invited to gather under the theme "One World under God." He wanted these religious leaders to affirm the dignity and value of each human being as a child of God and the central importance of establishing God-centered marriages and families. He hoped that they would return to their respective nations and encourage their followers to live these values out as well.

While promoting such interreligious initiatives, my father also clearly understood the unique position of Jesus as Lord and Savior. He spoke repeatedly about how Jesus' brief three years of ministry had shaped human history. He saw the United States, with its founding documents declaring God-given rights of freedoms of speech and religion, and its Bill of Rights limiting the power of government, as the fruit of Judeo-Christian teachings. He believed America was called to be a force for good in the world and frequently reiterated his gratitude to U.S. forces for liberating him from prison in Communist North Korea.

Because of the biblical teaching that all human beings have a common divine origin, America welcomes people of different faiths, or no faith, to exercise their freedom of conscience. Yet my father also saw that many Americans did not understand the real nature of the ideological and political threats to their nation and world.

For that reason, he expended enormous resources to educate citizens through establishing *The Washington Times* and newspapers in other nations, as well as hosting seminars critiquing and giving a counterproposal to the dialectical materialist theory of Communism. He strongly supported the election of Ronald Reagan and his Peace through Strength strategies. Reagan's policies led to the downfall of many Communist governments, thus liberating hundreds of millions of people from this tyranny.

My father also saw clearly the challenge of political Islam. There are many who would prefer to ignore this problem by censoring honest discussion. My father was unafraid to give voice to unpleasant truths.

****

To be clear, there are good and bad Christians, good and bad Jews and good and bad Muslims. Each one of us makes choices to do what is right or wrong every day of our lives. However, any honest discussion of these faiths must take into account essential differences in their worldviews.

Jim was the oldest of five children. He had
reported independently and objectively from

Recent Victims of Islamist Terrorism

We all know about the horrific attack on the World Trade Center on 9/11 that killed nearly 3,000 human beings. We also remember the beheading in Pakistan of Daniel Pearl, a journalist for the *Wall Street Journal* in **2002**, the beheading of James Foley, an American journalist, in Syria by members of ISIS in **2012**, the murders of 14 people in San Bernadino, California in **2015**, the murders of 49 people at a gay nightclub in Orlando, Florida in **2016**.

In France, 12 people were killed at the offices of the French satirical magazine *Charlie Hebdo* in January **2015**; 130 people were killed by suicide bombers in Paris in November **2015**. In Brussels, 32 civilians were killed in three suicide bombings in March **2016**. In July **2016**, 86 men, women and children were murdered and 458 others injured by Mohamed Lahouaiej-Bouhel, who drove a 19 ton truck into crowds of people walking on the street in Nice, France. These innocent victims were not killed by Buddhist monks, Catholic nuns, or Orthodox rabbis. They were murdered by Islamist extremists.

Photo credit: Rodi Said/Reuters Pictures

The greatest number of victims of political Islam, however, are those living under their direct control, such as the Yazidis in Syria, and other Muslims who have an "unacceptable" interpretation of the Quran. Christians who have lived in the Middle East for two thousand years have also been especially targeted for attack.

On Palm Sunday, 2017, Egypt's Coptic Christian community was hit by suicide bombers sent by the Islamic State, resulting in the deaths of 44 people.[1] That blood-soaked episode was an all-too-common instance of violent attacks against Middle Eastern Christians. Shortly thereafter, in Upper Egypt, gunmen attacked a convoy of Coptic Christians, resulting in 26 deaths. As reported in The New York Times, "the wave of persecution is still so severe that some fear it may bring about the end of Christianity in the region where it was born two millennia ago." [2-3]

While these barbarous acts are not representative of all Muslims, it would be foolish to ignore how widespread hatred and disregard for freedom of religion is in much of the Islamic world.

In 2014, a poll of 52,100 people in 102 countries found that 74% of North African and Middle Eastern residents expressed anti-Semitic hatred and beliefs.[4] Even in Muslim nations far removed from the Arab-Israeli conflict, majorities of their populations express such views. In majority-Muslim Malaysia, 61% harbor anti-Semitic attitudes, while only 13% of neighboring majority-Buddhist Thais are anti-Jewish.

Here in the U.S., Louis Farrakhan, leader of the Nation of Islam, expresses similar views, saying that Judaism is a "gutter religion" and that Adolf Hitler was a "great man."[5] I remember well how my father reached out to Mr. Farrakhan to help him and his followers embrace the fact that we are all God's children. Unfortunately, Farrakhan's words do not reflect that truth.

Honoring Murderers as "Heroes" and "Martyrs"

You might think that such prejudiced attitudes only reflect the views of ignorant, powerless people, but consider this- the Palestine Liberation Organization and the related Palestinian Authority consider the murderers of Jewish Israeli citizens to be martyrs. Consequently, the Palestinian Authority rewards families of the murderers.[6]

For example – in 2016, in a Hebron suburb, Mohammed Tarayra stabbed to death a 13-year-old Jewish girl, Hallel Yaffa Ariel, who was also an American citizen, as she was sleeping in her bed. As reported in Bloomberg News, "the stabbing was part of a seven month wave of attacks by Palestinians who shot,

Hallel Yaffa Ariel

stabbed, and ran down Jews with the encouragement of social media and popular songs."[7]

The ruling Fatah party in Palestine glorified the stabber, who was afterwards killed by security guards. On its official Facebook page, Taraya's mother told a local news outlet: "My son is a hero. He made me proud. My son died as a martyr defending Jerusalem and the Al-Aqsa Mosque."[8] The highest payments go to those assailants who manage to kill at least one Israeli, while the lowest go to those who didn't manage to kill or wound anyone.[9]

Do some Israelis commit heinous crimes against Muslim civilians? Unfortunately they do, but they are not honored by government officials as "martyrs." Their families are not sent payments for their murderous acts. Their families do not boast of them as "heroes." For example, three Israelis were convicted and given life sentences in Israeli courts for murdering a Palestinian, Mohammed Abu Khdeir, on July 2, 2014.[10]

Widespread Support for the Death Penalty for Those who Leave Islam

Troubling numbers of Muslims support the death penalty for those who choose to leave Islam, especially among those who support making Sharia the law of the land. Killing apostates is most widely supported in Egypt (86%) and Jordan (82%). According to the Pew Research Center, "roughly two-thirds who want Sharia to be the law of the land also back this penalty in the Palestinian territories."[11] In Malaysia and Pakistan, 62% support taking the life of Muslims who convert to another religion.[12] Similar numbers support stoning those who commit adultery, severely punishing those who criticize Muhammad or Islam, and chopping off hands for theft.

Support for such views is less prevalent among Muslims living in Central Asia and Europe. However, there is a wide gap between many adherents of the Islamic faith and members of the Jewish or Christian faiths. For Jews and Christians, even asking the question whether someone leaving their faith should be executed would be laughable.

Jesus and his disciples did not advocate converting people by force or punishing people who left the Christian faith with execution. Unfortunately, freedom of conscience is not part of the value system of many Islamists who want to establish a nation based on Sharia law.

Of course, not all Muslims fit into this extremist mold. To give one inspiring example:

Following the German occupation in 1943, the Muslim-majority nation of Albania refused to comply with Nazi orders to turn over lists of Jews residing within the country's borders. Various Albanian government agencies provided Jewish families with fake documentation that allowed them to intermingle amongst the rest of the population. Albanians also provided sanctuary to Jewish refugees who had arrived in their country, when it was still under Italian rule, risking deportation to concentration camps.[13]

A Short Summary of the Expansion of Political Islam

Many commentators criticize the Christian Crusades, which sought to take back the "Holy Land" from Muslim control. However, it's worth remembering that the Crusades arose in the late 11th century, after four centuries of relentless Islamic efforts to conquer Europe. Islam was being spread by military conquest and the sword.

The expansion of Islam began with Muhammad's active military leadership. As summarized by author Dan McLaughlin:

The fall of Mecca in 630 A.D. solidified Muhammad's control of the western side of the Arabian peninsula. A decisive Muslim victory at the Battle of Ajnadayn in 634 spread Muslim control into modern Israel. Between 634 and 689, Muslim forces conquered Christian, Byzantine-held Syria and North Africa.

Starting in the middle of the 7th century, Islamic incursions moved to Europe. Muslim armies conquered and attempted to conquer Spain, France, and Italy. Fighting raged from Constantinople in the east, to the frontiers of Georgia in the Caucasus, with the islands of the Mediterranean on the front lines.

Islamic efforts against Europe and the West continued well after the Crusades, from the fall of Constantinople in 1453 until the naval incursions finally stopped at Lepanto in 1571, to the epic Siege of Vienna in 1683 (which in turn was followed by another century of bloody wars between the Muslim Ottomans and Christian Hapsburgs).

As has often been noted, Muhammad's history as a military leader, and Islam as the driving force of conquest is a stark contrast with the early history of Christianity, a persecuted faith founded by a martyr who led no military campaigns. While Muslims do not possess an exclusive monopoly on imperialism, it is undeniable that the

Christian Crusades were a defensive response to centuries of Muslim expansion across formerly Christian and Jewish lands. Looking at its history, it is hard to argue that it has been a religion of "Peace."[14]

Reform Movements in the Islamic World

One ray of hope for the world is that there are Muslims who want to reform their faith and persuade others to reject the violence of Islamism, or "political Islam." One example is the Muslim Reform Movement,[15] which states that:

We are in a battle for the soul of Islam, and an Islamic renewal must defeat the ideology of Islamism, or politicized Islam, which seeks to create Islamic states, as well as an Islamic caliphate. Facing the threat of terrorism, intolerance, and social injustice in the name of Islam, we have reflected on how we can transform our communities based on three principles: peace, human rights, and secular governance. We consider all people equal with no birth rights other than human rights.

We reject blasphemy laws. They are a cover for the restriction of freedom of speech and religion. We affirm every individual's right to participate equally in ijtihad, or critical thinking.

We believe in freedom of religion and the right of all people to express and practice their faith, or non-faith, without threat of intimidation, persecution, discrimination or violence. Apostasy is not a crime. Our ummah–our community–is not just Muslims, but all of humanity.

The sad reality is that such reformers are literally risking their lives to bring change to the Islamic world. They deserve the support of all people of good will. It is shocking that many of these reformers are not welcome to speak at American universities.

One example is Hussein Aboubakr, a military instructor and researcher raised in Egypt who is calling for reform of Islam. In February 2015 he was yelled at, cursed at, and successfully prevented from speaking at Swarthmore College in Pennsylvania by students who had been led to believe that any criticism of Islam is unacceptable.[16]

Another example is Ayaan Hirsi Ali, a Somali-born former Dutch lawmaker. She was offered an honorary degree for her advocacy work on behalf of women and girls in Muslim societies by Brandeis University, only to have it withdrawn due to pressure from students, faculty activists and pressure groups like the Council for American-Islamic Relations. An avid critic of the ties between violence and fundamentalist Islam, she constantly speaks out against forced child marriages, female genital mutilation, and "honor killings" of girls or women perceived to have brought dishonor on their family. The reason for withdrawing her invitation to speak and her honorary degree? Telling painful, politically incorrect truths based on her own direct, personal knowledge.

One professor of African studies accused her of spewing "antiquated, racist logics that present people from the Middle East and Africa as culturally backward and in need of the civilizing influences of the West." [17] So rather than deal with the reality of female genital mutilation, forced child marriages and honor killings, let's just "kill the messenger," or at a minimum prevent her from telling Brandeis students the ugly truth about the oppression of women and girls in much of the Islamic world.

Silencing of European Critics of Islam

In much of Europe, this silencing of honest discussions about political Islam is even worse. As reported by the Gatestone Institute:

In France, those who criticize Islam - or who just show the results of Islamic terrorism - are victims of fierce prosecution.

In March 2018, French President Macron said he wanted a law against "fake news". If his plan is adopted into law, all online magazines in France that do not broadcast what the government defines as "true news" could be subject to immediate government suspension. If the online publications originate outside France, access to them would be blocked. Islamic online magazines and websites are not on the proposed list of "fake news" providers. What online magazines and websites would top the list? Those that question Islam.

After the terrorist attacks that took place in France in November 2015 and in July 2016, journalists and writers who stated that terrorists attacking France were Muslim, and that "Islamism" was not foreign to Islam, were prosecuted in court and fined thousands of Euros.[18]

In Sweden, the situation is just as serious. According to a 2015 Gatestone Institute report:

Forty years after the Swedish parliament unanimously decided in 1975 to change the formerly homogenous Sweden into a multicultural country, violent crime has increased by 300%. Sweden is now number two on the list of rape countries, surpassed only by Lesotho in Southern Africa.

In 1975, 421 rapes were reported to the Swedish police; in 2014, it was 6,620. That is an increase of 1,472%, even though the population only grew by 19% during those 4 decades.[19]

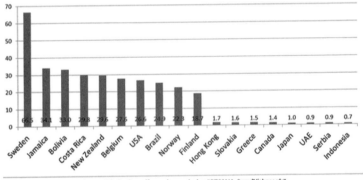

Rape at the national level, number of police-recorded offences (rate/100,000) - United nations (2012)

Source: United nations office on drugs and crime "CTS2013_SexualViolence.xls"

In response to this horrific rise of rapes, Michael Hess, a local politician from the Sweden Democrat Party, encouraged Swedish journalists to get acquainted with Islam's view of women who do not dress according to its standards:

"When will you journalists realize that it is deeply rooted in Islam's

culture to rape and brutalize women who refuse to comply with Islamic teachings? There is a strong connection between rapes in Sweden and the number of immigrants from MENA-countries [Middle East and North Africa]."

This remark led to Michael Hess being charged with the crime of "denigration of ethnic groups." In May 2017, he was handed a suspended jail sentence and a fine.

For many years, Mr. Hess lived in Muslim countries, and is well acquainted with Islam and its view of women. During his trial, he provided evidence of how Sharia law deals with rape, and statistics to indicate that Muslims are the main perpetrators of rape in Sweden. However, the court decided that the facts were irrelevant.

In an astounding number of cases, Swedish courts have demonstrated sympathy for the rapists, and have acquitted suspects who have claimed that the girl wanted to have sex with six, seven or eight men.

The internet radio station Granskning Sverige called the mainstream newspapers Aftonbladet and Expressen to ask why they had described the perpetrators as "Swedish men" when they actually were Somalis without Swedish citizenship. These journalists were hugely offended when asked if they felt any responsibility to warn Swedish women to stay away from certain men. One journalist asked "why that should be their responsibility?" [20]

The nation of Germany, which has accepted more than a million immigrants from MENA countries in recent years, has also seen a rise in rapes of German women who do not dress according to Sharia standards. One infamous incident took place on New Year's Eve 2016 in Cologne, where "scores of young women" were "groped and robbed" by "gangs of men described by authorities as having North African or Arabic" appearance. *The New York Times* reported that "hundreds of young men broke into groups and formed rings around young women, refusing to let them escape...The women who were attacked screamed and tried to fight their way free, a man who had struggled to protect his girlfriend told German public television." [21]

Equally disturbing are reports that Germany's Federal Office for Refugees and Migration has been rejecting almost all asylum requests from converts from Islam to Christianity, according to Thomas Schirrmacher, president of the International Society for Human Rights. He said that when undergoing "belief tests," [the Federal Office for Refugees and Migration] often relies on Muslim translators who deliberately mistranslate at the expense of Christians or converts. "It is a scandal that almost all converts from Islam to Christianity are being denied asylum," Schirrmacher said. [22]

Solving the very real challenges of absorbing large numbers of immigrants from Islamic countries and how to assimilate them into Western culture is not helped by suppressing honest discussion of these issues. Leftist "progressives" and feminists take pride in claiming that they stand for human rights, but their silence about the oppression of women and girls in the Islamic world, and the justification for rape of women who refuse to comply with Islamic teachings is deafening. It is also reminiscent of their silence regarding the mass murders committed under Communism. Their willingness to use government power to punish politically incorrect statements should be alarming to anyone who cares about free speech.

Reformers who risk their lives to challenge political Islam and improve the lives of those who have been victimized by it, deserve the support of all people of good will--not the slander and ostracism they have experienced throughout the world.

6
Our Judeo-Christian Foundation Protects Freedom for All

In In the 16th century, a bald-headed monk claimed that Christians could communicate directly with God and did not need the papacy to intercede for them. Just as the martyr John Hus had proclaimed 100 years earlier, Martin Luther declared that it was Scripture, the Word of God, which deserved that coveted central position:[1]

Unless I am convinced by the testimony of the Scriptures or by clear reason (for I do not trust either in the pope or in councils alone, since it is well-known that they have often erred and contradicted themselves), I am bound by the Scriptures. I have quoted and my conscience is captive to the Word of God. I cannot and will not recant anything, since it is neither safe nor right to go against conscience.[2]

Luther's belief in the priesthood of all believers gave rise to a new paradigm of relationship between individuals and the hierarchical structures they inhabited. By nailing his 95 Theses to the door of the Castle Church in Wittenberg, Germany, Martin Luther unleashed a spiritual tidal wave which shifted the foundation of Christian faith away from the centralized authority of the Catholic Church to the individual. The world of political thinkers such as John Locke, whose ideas on religious freedom were a major influence on the drafters of the U.S.

Constitution, was in large measure shaped by Luther's actions more than a century before.[3]

While the Founding Fathers adhered to a variety of religious beliefs, the majority held the conviction that they did not want to be controlled by a king.

It was not just the English King's authority the Founding Fathers were rejecting, it was the authority of centralized power itself. Whether Christian or Deist, they were all thoroughly aware of the Biblical culture and its stories. To give an example, John Adams, who later became the 2nd president of the United States, wrote to a fellow compatriot in 1776:

The management of so complicated and mighty a machine, as the United Colonies, requires the Meekness of Moses, the Patience of Job and the Wisdom of Solomon, added to the Valor of Daniel.[4]

Why did the founders insist upon the division of powers into executive, legislative and judicial branches? They had experienced what centralized tyranny was like and wanted none of the "divine" right of kings that was common in Europe. But they were also familiar with the Biblical perspective that all men and women had become sinful as a result of the Fall and thus structured American government with checks and balances to protect against the human tendency for corruption.

The founders limited the scope of the national government for the same reason. All powers not expressly given to the federal government were reserved to the states and local governmental bodies.

Some of the founders owned slaves, a national sin that led to the bloodiest war in American history. However, the principles enunciated in the Declaration of Independence were the ones in the mouths of the abolitionists who demanded an end to slavery.

They were quoted by Martin Luther King nearly two centuries later when he spoke at the Washington Monument in 1963:

In a sense we've come to our nation's capital to cash a check. When the architects of our Republic wrote the magnificent words of the Constitution and the Declaration of Independence, they were signing• a promissory note to which every American was to fall heir. This note was a promise that all men—yes, black men as well as white men—would be guaranteed the unalienable rights of life, liberty and the pursuit of happiness.

Why is America a "land of opportunity?"

Over the past century, many millions of immigrants from all over the world have left their homelands to come to this country, seeing it as the "land of opportunity." Why is America a place of prosperity? Its constitutional republic form of government, even with its often "messy" politics, is emulated by nations all over the world.

Why do so many countries, which try to copy the external form of American democracy, fail to become prosperous and vibrant themselves?

The framers knew that a shared culture rooted in Judeo-Christian values was necessary for the republican form of government to work. As John Adams put it:

We have no government armed with powers capable of contending with human passions unbridled by morality and religion. Avarice, ambition, revenge or gallantry would break the strongest cords of our Constitution as a whale goes through a net. Our Constitution was made only for a moral and religious people. It is wholly inadequate to the government of any other.[5]

As explained by Professor Edward Lynch of Hollins University, for a constitutional republic to work, it needs three things: trust, hope and a sense that "I have power to make improvements in my life and in the lives of those I care about."[6]

Corruption, however, destroys all of these things. In order for corruption to thrive it requires human greed, a monopoly of power, and anonymity. Removing the first element is a personal choice, but governments can do a lot, for good or for ill, regarding the last two. Lynch argues that the persistence of poverty and dysfunction in many "democracies" around the world has to do with centralization of power. Dictatorships and oligarchies breed corruption, since they can easily hide their decisions behind a veil of anonymity.[7]

For example, Peruvian sociologist Hernando De Soto decided to compare the challenges of starting a business in Lima, Peru with starting one in Miami, Florida. He was able to complete and file all the required permits for a new business in Miami in one day. In Lima, it took 14 months. Without paying three essential bribes, it would not have been possible to start the business at all.[8]

It is easy to see in which country someone would be more willing to take the risk of starting a new business. Centralized government fosters corruption and sabotages trust and initiative.

Decentralized power allows for more competition. If one locality is corrupt, a person can simply move their business elsewhere. Since most decisions are being made at the local level, anonymity is less of a problem. You are much more likely to know who is making those decisions.

Americans are known for their independence and initiative, which allows them to try (and fail) to build new enterprises, charities, churches and businesses.

The Parable of the Talents in Matthew 25 can be seen as a story about entrepreneurship. A man going on a journey called his servants and entrusted them with bags of silver. The first two servants doubled what they had been given, and were praised by their master. The third servant buried the one bag of silver he had been given, and was judged harshly by his master for not making any effort to increase it.

We cannot control the circumstances of our birth, but we are responsible for what we do with what we've been given.

Madam C. J. Walker (1867-1919) is a great example. As described by the History Channel, she was lauded as "the first black woman millionaire in America" for her successful line of hair care products. Born Sarah Breedlove, she was widowed by age 20 and went to work as a laundress. After seeking treatment for hair loss, she developed the "Walker system" and sold her homemade products directly to black women. A talent for self-promotion helped build a booming enterprise. Walker funded scholarships for women at the Tuskegee Institute and donated large sums to the NAACP, the black YMCA and dozens of other charities.[9]

Progressivism- Return to a Failed Model

The 20th century progressive political movement in the U.S., as described in chapter 4, is a return to the centralized model that America's founders rejected. By centralizing power in the hands of a few, people are incentivized to look to big government to solve their problems. Rather than dealing with difficulties in their communities, people instead compete for resources and benefits distributed from Washington, D.C.

Funding and regulating education was another activity the founders never envisioned for the federal government. There is little proof that increased government spending on education has improved student outcomes. Progressives in America have virtually total control of the American public school system and the results are evident. While America used to lead the world in academic standards, our students now lag far behind many countries in reading, math, and science scores. It is worth noting that some of the countries scoring in the top tier were quite impoverished as recently as 30 years ago.[10] Students graduate from high school knowing less about American history than their grandparents did.[11] This is more evidence that government-controlled education is not working very well for many of America's youth. Furthermore, while the Founding Fathers were opposed to a state-funded or authorized church, they did not envision a public sphere or government that was sterilized of any reference to the Creator or Judeo-Christian teachings.

This is apparent in Ben Franklin's recommendation for the nation's Great Seal, which depicted the scene described in the book of Exodus, where the Israelites confronted the Pharoah of Egypt in order to gain their freedom. The motto encircling the seal read: *"Rebellion to Tyrants is Obedience to God."*

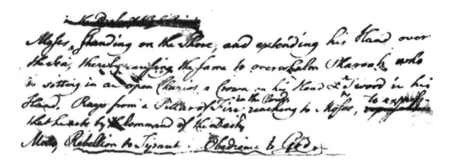

Moses ~~in the Dress of a High Priest~~[*] standing on the Shore, and extending his Hand over the Sea, thereby causing the same to over-whelm Pharoah   who is sitting in an open Chariot, a Crown on his Head & a[b] Sword in his Hand. Rays from a Pillar of Fire in the Clouds[c] reaching to Moses, ~~expressing~~ to express that he acts by ~~the~~ Command of the Deity

   Motto, *Rebellion to Tyrants is Obedience to God.*

* The words "in the Dress of a High Priest" are inserted with a caret and deleted.
b The article "a" is inserted with a caret.
c The words "in the Clouds" are inserted with a caret.

Transcription of Ben Franklin's handwritten description of his Great Seal design (1776)

Free from Government Control

Thomas Jefferson's belief in the separation of church and state is often mistakenly understood as a belief that the public sphere should be religion-free. Jefferson was not a Christian in the traditional sense, but he believed that Jesus' teachings constituted the "outlines of a system of the most sublime morality which has ever fallen from the lips of man." [12]Along with many of his contemporaries, he objected to the fact that in some colonies, ministers were mandated to preach according to the doctrine established by the Church of England. Citizens were often required by law to attend church on Sunday. Taxes were created to provide wages for church ministers, as well as for the construction of new churches.

Maryland had passed an "Act of Toleration" law in 1649 which allowed Catholics to practice their faith, but also imposed the death penalty for Jews and atheists who did not believe in Christ[13] Jefferson understood that government had no business getting involved in people's relationship with their Creator; it had no right to impose bureaucratic, punitive dictates onto its citizens:

The rights of conscience we never submitted, we could not submit. We are answerable for them to our God. The legitimate powers of government extend to such acts only as are injurious to others. But it does me no injury for my neighbour to say there are twenty gods, or no god. It neither picks my pocket nor breaks my leg...[14]

Foremost in Jefferson's mind was the creation of a society which allowed for diversity of religious thought, free from any and all governmental control.

But do we see diversity of thought being freely expressed in the public sphere? Rather than allowing for individual expression, the government has become more and more of a repressive regime, curtailing religious speech and promoting its own secular state religion. Nearly all public schools in the United States are Bible-free zones, but children as young as kindergarten are free to choose their gender any day of the week.

A shocking example of the abuse of state power can be seen in the recent "student protest" demanding stricter gun laws. In March 2018, tens of thousands of public school students across the United States convened in outdoor rallies to demand stricter gun laws.

This was no academic exercise; the rally was a bold

manipulation of students' emotions by redirecting their anguish at school shootings into hostility towards defenders of the Second Amendment.

Youth from public schools were hand-picked by the organizers to blame lawful gun-owners and an organization working to protect their rights, the National Rifle Association. Was effort made to provide opposing points of view, such as the utter failure of government institutions to prevent or stop the Parkland school shooter? No.

Where you stand on the gun debate is not the point here. The issue is whether government-regulated and funded schools have the right to promote the talking-points of one political party.

The truth is, America cannot maintain freedom without holding fast to her Judeo-Christian values, from which comes the conviction that you and I are equals, regardless of our sex, skin color, nationality, or religion. The belief that we have a common Heavenly Father, who created us with free will, is the strongest basis for treating people of other backgrounds as equals. The Founding Fathers recognized this, and created a Constitution which limits the state's power to control or manipulate religious practice, while giving freedom to U.S. citizens to worship as they choose.

My father taught extensively that God and strong families, not the state, are the building blocks for peaceful communities, peaceful nations and a peaceful world. The truth is, "multicultural" teachings that encourage free sex, victimhood, blame and envy are greater threats to our nation than any foreign invader.

America was once a culture where the Ten Commandments

were respected as a higher truth all citizens should try to live by. Today, it has veered away from the foundation upon which its shared civic culture was built. We must not stand idly by while our country's unifying purpose is being destroyed. We owe it to our descendants to ensure that the Founders' heritage is passed on to them and to future generations in the years to come.

7
He Shall Rule Them with a Rod Of Iron

Jesus' Gospel is the Gospel of the Kingdom

The "Good News" has traditionally been explained as exclusively the Crucifixion, Death and Resurrection of Jesus Christ. But what does Jesus say about the Good News? A close look at the words of Christ reveals that his Gospel is the Gospel of the Kingdom. In the book of Matthew alone, Christ preaches the message of the coming Kingdom over forty times to the crowds that gather around him.

In contrast, he speaks of his imminent crucifixion on only three occasions, privately, to his inner circle of disciples.

Throughout the New Testament, Jesus' preaching centers on the message of God's sovereign reign:

> *From that time Jesus began to preach, and to say, "Repent: for the kingdom of heaven is at hand."* Matthew 4:17

> *And Jesus went about all Galilee, teaching in their synagogues, and preaching the gospel of the kingdom, and healing all manner of sickness and all manner of disease among the people.* Matthew 4:23

> *And as ye go, preach, saying, "The kingdom of heaven is at hand."* Matthew 10:7

And this gospel of the kingdom shall be preached in all the world for a witness unto all nations; and then shall the end come. Matthew 24:14

Then shall the King say unto them on his right hand, Come, ye blessed of my Father, inherit the kingdom prepared for you from the foundation of the world... Matthew 25:34

Now after that John was put in prison, Jesus came into Galilee, preaching the gospel of the kingdom of God... Mark 1:14

In Matthew 6:33, Jesus makes it clear that before we do anything else, before we worry about tomorrow, we need to first seek God's Kingdom. Jesus didn't say, "Seek ye first democracy." He didn't say, "Seek ye first communism." He didn't say, "Seek ye first some useless diploma." He said, "Seek ye first the kingdom, and his righteousness, and all these things shall be added unto you."

In Matthew 9:35, Jesus went about all the cities and villages, teaching in the synagogues, preaching the Gospel of the Kingdom, and healing every disease among the people.

In Luke 4:43, Jesus said to the people:"I must preach the kingdom of God to other cities also: for therefore am I sent." He did not say that he was sent to preach the Gospel of the Crucifixion, or the Gospel of Death, or the Gospel of the Resurrection on the third day. On the contrary, Jesus said he was sent for the purpose of preaching the Kingdom of God.

Jesus also made it clear that his Kingdom was to be physical as well as spiritual: "Our Father which art in Heaven, hallowed be thy name. **Thy kingdom come**, thy will be done **on Earth** as it is in Heaven." (Matthew 6:9-10) It will not just be a celestial Kingdom, a place to enter only after we die. Christ's Kingdom will be a Kingdom with justice and goodness that Christ will usher onto this earth.

The Rod of Iron

Because we live in the time of the Last Days, the promise of the Kingdom is now being fulfilled. Many are receiving revelations and inspirations from the Holy Spirit. Jesus will come with a new name (see Revelation 3:12), and he will establish a reign where good people, along with Christ, will rule with the Rod of Iron:

> *Ask me, and I will make the nations your inheritance, the ends of the earth your possession. You will break them with a rod of iron; you will dash them to pieces like pottery.*
> Psalm 2:8-9

> *And he shall rule them with a rod of iron; as the vessels of a potter shall they be broken to shivers: even as I received of my Father.* Revelation 2:27

> *And she brought forth a man child, who was to rule all nations with a rod of iron: and her child was caught up unto God, and to his throne.* Revelation 12:5

> *And out of his mouth goeth a sharp sword, that with it he should smite the nations: and he shall rule them with a rod of iron: and he treadeth the winepress of the fierceness and wrath of Almighty God.* Revelation 19:15

When Christ returns, he will be the ruler whose words will judge the nations.

When John wrote the book of Revelation, the sword was the common weapon of war. It was the means by which sovereigns maintained their positions of power; it secured satanic rule over their monarchies. For God's Kingdom to come on earth, godly people, centered on Christ, must be able to wield stronger "fire-power" than the forces of evil (see Revelation chapter 20). The scriptures from the last book of the New Testament portray the Rod of Iron as a prominent accoutrement, an essential physical item demonstrating how Christ will govern when he returns. His Kingdom is kept safe and maintained by the just use of the Rod of Iron. In the book of Revelation chapter 20, Christ uses the power of fire (or "firepower") against the wicked who are "as many as the sands of the sea" to cast Satan into the lake of fire for punishment.

But for modern day people, it is often difficult to associate Christ with weapons; the two entities may seem to appear mutually exclusive. In addition, people are naturally afraid of firearms because of their lethal force. An object causing death tends to evoke a knee-jerk reaction, often resulting in the belief that no civilian should possess a gun. "Pacifist" believers may claim that God alone controls the power over life and death. But that assertion begs the question: how can God, who is invisible, control weapons? How does that work in real life?

We don't have to look too far to see that when godly people lack the power to defend themselves, evil runs amuck. Centralized government, for example, has murdered over two hundred twenty million *unarmed civilians* in the last 100 years, many of whom were killed for their faith in God.

Orthodox Christian author and Russian dissident Alexander Solzhenitsyn was a man who experienced firsthand the misery created by centralized government, spending eight years as a prisoner in the gulag labor camps created by Josef Stalin. Solzhenitsyn was a Russian literary giant who, when describing the main reason for the sixty million Russian deaths caused by Communism stated simply: "Men have forgotten

God; that's why all this has happened."[1]

Christians Recognize a Higher Authority

As Christians, we understand that Satan has used the power of the state to dominate, enslave, and murder God's children. Christianity especially is perceived as a threat to the state's identity, because Christianity elevates the value of the individual. It creates a bond among people, fostering solidarity and helping those in need. Governments rightly fear that Christianity will become a channel through which social revolts can gain strength.

When studying the life and lessons of Jesus, the Scriptures reveal teachings that are antithetical to state allegiance. Although Jesus held no political office during his lifetime, he was nonetheless considered potentially dangerous to the Roman Empire. Herod the Great unintentionally confirmed the validity of Jesus' position as "King of the Jews" when he gave the decree to massacre all young male children at the time of the Savior's birth. In the first three Gospels, Christ repeatedly spoke of God's impending monarchical rule. Assertions that Jesus was the embodiment of God and King of the Jews were key factors in the hostile response he received from both the Jewish and Roman hierarchies.

Jesus was a true revolutionary who shocked and angered the Jewish ruling elite by his proclamations that he alone was the sovereign worthy of their allegiance. Following him meant they would have to honor a rebel rabbi above their Roman superiors. This shift in allegiance would have placed the Jewish leaders in a precarious, life-threatening situation. Rome dealt swiftly and decisively with potential uprisings. The state did not hesitate to employ torture and crucifixion as a regular practice when dealing with slaves or rebels. A miracle-working, charismatic Jewish prophet who was able to mobilize large crowds could easily be perceived as a threat to the status quo.

Jesus Did Not Reject the Use of Force

To say that Jesus was a pacifist is inaccurate. He manufactured his own force-multiplying weapon when he made his whip to assault and chase out the greedy, self-serving money changers in the Temple.

Jesus affirmed the right to military grade defensive arms in Luke 22:36 when he said to his disciples:

> *Then said he unto them, But now, he that hath a purse, let him take it, and likewise his scrip: and he that hath no sword, let him sell his garment, and buy one.*

Jesus suggested his support for the death penalty when he said in Matthew 18:6:

> *But who so shall offend one of these little ones which believe in me, it were better for him that a millstone were hanged about his neck, and that he were drowned in the depth of the sea.*

The truth is, Jesus posed a threat to Jewish and Roman leadership with his gospel of the Kingdom. They became increasingly angry and threatened by his message, because it was a message that was overturning their centralized power.

In this time of the Second Coming, what kind of ruler can we expect Jesus to be when he returns? Some Christians are wondering if the Kingdom of God will usher in a time when humanity will be kept in subjection by a divine dictatorship. Some have intimated that the reign of Christ will be overtly oppressive, a place where the King of Kings reigns by subjecting all peoples to the absolute will of God. Perhaps, secretly, some Christians have privately thought that it would be better to live in a free America than in the Kingdom of God, which they assume will be one of totalitarian rule!

The Shepherd Willing to Risk His Life

However, when we examine the Greek word used for "rule" in Revelation, the Bible indicates that when Christ returns, he will have the same character as before. As mentioned in chapter 2, the Greek word *poimaino* is the word used to refer to Christ's rule in the rod of iron passages in Revelation. The Rod of Iron rule is a *poimaino* rule. *Poimaino* means literally to act as a shepherd, not a dictator. A shepherd tends, herds, guards, and guides. A good shepherd does not want to terrorize his sheep; he uses his rod to protect them from harm or danger —"thy rod and thy staff, they comfort me (Psalm 23).

Poimaino rule is a caring rule, centered on a God who is just and merciful. Jesus, the King of Kings, who knows his flock, will still be the good shepherd in the Kingdom —for the Bible says, *"Jesus Christ is the same yesterday, today and forever"* (Hebrews 13:8). God is a protective Father who wants His children to be strong so that the forces of evil cannot destroy them.

To overcome wickedness, there must appear good, moral people who are firm and unyielding in defending justice. Only the Rod of Iron gives Christ's followers the ability to say "no" to tyrants.

There have been endless cycles of human suffering, of people being ruled and "tax-farmed" time and time again by centralized governments, aristocracies, and "above the law" elite superclasses.

Unlike monarchies of the past, however, God's Kingdom is an upside-down Kingdom. It is radically different. In the Kingdom of God, the formerly "poor in spirit" and those who were slaves and serfs will inherit his Kingdom authority and power, to be co-rulers along with him (see Matthew 5). Christ never meant to rule as a totalitarian, and while he reigns as the head, we are to be co-heirs of the Kingdom:

> *For ye have not received the spirit of bondage again to fear; but ye have received the Spirit of adoption, whereby we cry, Abba, Father.*
>
> *The Spirit itself beareth witness with our spirit, that we are the children of God:*
>
> *And if children, then heirs; heirs of God, and joint-heirs with Christ; if so be that we suffer with him, that we may be also glorified together.* Romans 8:15-17

To share in the sufferings and glory of Jesus means that we spend our lives "putting on Christ" (see Romans 13:14), and become those people who can be trusted to exercise great power with love and mercy, as well as with firmness and justice.

In his Sermon on the Mount, Jesus was not just teaching individual followers; he was also educating humanity about the culture of the inheritors of the coming Kingdom:

> *Blessed are the poor in spirit: for theirs is the kingdom of heaven.*
>
> *Blessed are they that mourn: for they shall be comforted.*
>
> *Blessed are the meek: for they shall inherit the earth.*
>
> *Blessed are they which do hunger and thirst after*

righteousness: for they shall be filled.

Blessed are the merciful: for they shall obtain mercy.

Blessed are the pure in heart: for they shall see God.

Blessed are the peacemakers: for they shall be called the children of God.

Blessed are they which are persecuted for righteousness' sake: for theirs is the kingdom of heaven.

Blessed are ye, when men shall revile you, and persecute you, and shall say all manner of evil against you falsely, for my sake.

Rejoice, and be exceeding glad: for great is your reward in heaven: for so persecuted they the prophets which were before you. Matthew 5:3-12

With his timeless wisdom, Jesus was teaching us the traits needed for a Kingdom of sovereign, armed people. Humility, compassion, mercy, purity, righteousness- these are Kingdom virtues. The Kingdom of Heaven, then, utilizes the Rod of Iron within the Christian framework. The Rod of Iron can only be used to properly maintain the Kingdom by moral Christ-aspiring citizens. Founding Fathers such as Charles Carroll understood this point:

Without morals, a republic cannot subsist any length of time; they therefore who are decrying the Christian religion, whose morality is so sublime and pure...are undermining the solid foundation of morals, the best security of free governments. [2]

The citizens of the Kingdom of God, who will share in Christ's sovereignty, bear the responsibility to defend their family, neighbors, and nation with their own rod of iron.

Those carrying the rod of iron are called to undergo spiritual as well as physical training, so that they may embody these kingdom values on both individual and national levels. It is only in this manner that a moral republic can be maintained. Our ability to prosper as armed defenders is contingent upon ongoing training and learning, with a radical dependence on Christ, who alone is the complete embodiment of the Gospel.

The Rod of Iron enables citizens of the Kingdom to maintain peace through strength. Christ's co-heirs become protectors of the Kingdom, staying strong through self-restraint and being slow to anger. Those bearing weapons must maintain a high level of discipline and vigilance. It is essential to learn how to master oneself, because the citizens have tremendous power when they bear the rod of iron. Once a bullet is fired it can never be taken back.

Every responsible parent has a natural instinct to protect his or her children at the risk of their own lives. God's Kingdom manifests a culture where we are our neighbor's "keeper." The Rod of Iron is the most effective way for someone of weaker stature, older in age, or handicapped to maintain his or her regal sovereignty. The fundamental principles of the Rod of Iron culture are loving God and loving our neighbor.

The armed citizen has the ability to say "NO!" to the evildoers, tyrants and those animated by the forces of Satan. Only an armed citizen can say, "NO! You cannot dominate me, kill me, control me, enslave me, rape me or enact evil upon me or my people. If you try to use lethal force upon me I will respond with lethal force to defend myself, my loved ones, or my kingdom."

As part of God's family, and sharing in Christ's sovereignty, the citizens of God's Kingdom wear their royal crowns with pride. Our allegiance is to God in Christ, not to the god of the state. This is why Jesus said: *"Hold on to what you have, so that no one will take away your crown."* (Revelation 3:11)

In putting on our crowns, we oppose all godless tyrannies, and stand as citizens of the Kingdom of God.

The 18th century American rebel spirit was infused with the sentiment that the colonists served but one monarch. As a British-appointed governor noted:

If you ask an American, who is his master? He will tell you he has none, nor any governor but Jesus Christ.[3]

Likewise, when British Major Pitcairn shouted to an assembled regiment of Minutemen: "Disperse, ye villains, lay down your arms in the name of George the Sovereign King of England" Rev. Jonas Clark responded:

We recognize no Sovereign but God and no King but Jesus![4]

Although America has seriously strayed from her godly roots, God has not let go of this special nation. It is because the American Revolution was centered on noble values that Americans still have the right to bear arms. The purpose for which we use something determines if God or Satan has power over it. Weapons are power, or force multipliers. When we use guns for a righteous purpose, such as freedom from tyranny and protection of liberty, then God has authority over them.

The reason why Christ gives us the ends of the earth for our possession in Psalm 2:8 is not so we can be egoists, but so we can exercise responsible stewardship on his behalf. When men and women of God have the earth as their possession, bearing the Rod of Iron, the wicked tyrants of the world will have to fear. "Sheepdogs" bearing arms bring consternation to the wolves, but they bring comfort to the sheep. They shield the people who know God and recognize His voice.

As children of God, we are called to take dominion over the Rod of Iron, not to idolize it. We are grateful for the accoutrements of the Crown and the Rod of Iron, given to us by God, but we do not worship them. We worship God, and we are grateful for the sovereignty and authority He has given to us.

8
Legal Gun Ownership Saves Lives

For every complex problem there is an answer that is clear, simple, and wrong. H.L. Mencken

With amazing rapidity, student survivors from the Stoneman Douglas high school shooting such as David Hogg, Emma Gonzalez and Cameron Kasky gave impassioned speeches heard on nationwide media, like National Public Radio, ABC News, CNN, many other cable TV channels, and at the March 24 "March for Our Lives." [1]

Kasky spoke of a "revolution" that is "powerful because it is, of, by and for the young people of this country." He warned:

Politicians, either represent the people or get out. The people demand the ban of assault weapons. The people demand we prohibit the sale of high capacity magazines. Stand with us or beware. The voters are coming. [2]

David Hogg accused gun store owners and legislators who support the 2nd Amendment of being:

...sick f*ckers [who] want to continue to sell more guns, murder more children, and honestly just get reelected. What kind of shitty person does that? They could have blood from children splattered all over their faces and they wouldn't take action, because all they still see are these dollar signs. [3]

Another student accuses "national policymakers (who) value the blood money of the NRA over the lives of children." [4]

The possibility that the "people" have a wide range of views on gun legislation and that legislators might have a principled reason for supporting the 2nd Amendment does not seem to occur to these teenagers. In their eyes, advocates for the 2nd Amendment are not just wrong, they are evil. These teenagers' claim to speak on behalf of "the people" is frankly reminiscent of the language of the 18th century French revolutionaries before mass executions of "enemies of the people."

Remembering my own opinionated youth, I am willing to give these young people a pass, but what about the adults behind them? Leftist politicians like N.Y. Senator Chuck Schumer are surely breaking out the champagne bottles as they see a generation of young voters persuaded to believe that all Republicans are evil politicians in the pocket of gun-loving advocacy groups. At the March 24th rally, Schumer said:

Every time, the viselike grip of the NRA on the necks of some of these politicians has succeeded, but this time it won't. You know why it won't? Because we have YOU! [5]

Schumer proudly pointed out that he authored the Brady Law and the assault weapons ban- but did gun registration and the "assault weapons ban" succeed in saving any lives? When we examine the research in this chapter, you will see that the answer is "No."

What about other students from Stoneman Douglas who were not allowed to speak at the CNN townhall, or at the "March for Our Lives," or on National Public Radio, because they disagreed with the pro-gun control narrative?

Take for example, Kyle Kashuv, who is also a survivor of the Parkland, Florida high school massacre. On CBS' "Face the Nation" he said,

And what I saw at the march yesterday which really frustrated me is that I have a different point of view, but what really concerned me was that how come I wasn't invited to speak at the march because as Americans we all have different point of views. And it's important to represent them all equally.

Kashuv argues that a ban on "assault weapons" and high capacity magazines will not solve the issue. Instead, he blamed the mass killing on law enforcement's failures to enforce existing laws and practices. He concluded:

And I find it ironic that after all this and we've seen so many different government failures, we want to trust the government even more.[6]

All of these students are full of passion, but when it comes to making real public policy and laws that will govern our lives, don't adults have the responsibility to do what is both constitutional and effective to reduce incidents of violence? Isn't it important for schools, which endorsed events like the "Student Walkout" on March 24 to have a wide variety of views expressed instead of one-sided rallies that could be interpreted as weaponizing youth passions for political purposes?

Ban "Assault Weapons"?

At the top of the "more gun control" agenda is bringing back a ban on "assault weapons." As David Hogg's words above indicate, gun owners and elected officials who question this are called "sick f*ckers [who] want to continue to sell more guns, murder more children, and honestly just get reelected."

Legislators who support the 2nd Amendment are accused of succumbing to the "viselike grip of the NRA on [their] necks," rather than representing the views of many of their constituents who use guns responsibly.

California Congressman Eric Swalwell called for banning possession of semiautomatic "assault" weapons, buying back such weapons from all who choose to abide by that new law, and criminally prosecuting "any who choose to defy it by keeping their weapons." [7]

Georgia Congresswoman Erica Thomas also supports banning "assault rifles" and then denies that these would be seized from lawful gun owners, even though a bill she supported as a Georgia legislator states, "The Georgia Bureau of Investigation *shall seize and take possession of* any assault weapon, large capacity magazine, armor piercing bullet or incendiary fifty caliber bullet." [8] Her doublespeak is typical and also shows ignorance about research conducted by the U.S. Department of Justice.

California Senator Feinstein and other gun control advocates urgently advocate the renewal of the federal "Assault Weapon Ban" law that was passed in 1994 and expired in 2004. The law prohibited the manufacture and sale of semiautomatic rifles with "military-style features" such as pistol grips as well as magazines holding more than 10 rounds of ammunition. However, a 2004 Department of Justice-funded study found no evidence that it had reduced overall gun crime or made shootings less lethal. This should not be surprising, since only about 3% of homicides are committed with rifles (including semiautomatic ones like AR-15s), while two thirds of all gun-related crimes are committed with handguns. [9] In 8 out of 10 gun crime cases, the perpetrator was not a lawful gun owner. The "law" obviously makes little difference to criminals.[10]

These are some of the "inconvenient truths" that gun control advocates are careful not to mention.

"Gun-Free Zones" – Free Except for Criminals' Guns

As pointed out by the Crime Prevention Research Center, during the past six decades, 98.4% of mass public shootings have taken place in "Gun-Free Zones," where the legal use of firearms is not permitted. Looking at the nearly two decades from 1998 to 2015, 96% of mass public shootings have taken place in such "weapon-free" areas.[11]

It is very apparent that this widespread approach to "reduce the number of guns" in such locations as schools, commercial areas, public open spaces, government properties, houses of worship, and health care facilities, by establishing "gun-free zones" has not worked. On the contrary, it works very well for criminals looking for a place where law-abiding citizens are forbidden to carry firearms. Having an armed security guard provides some protection, but knowing the exact location of such a person often makes him an easy target.

For example, the diary of the Batman movie theater killer, James Holmes, who murdered 12 people and injured 70 others in 2012 in Aurora, Colorado, reveals that he was debating between attacking an airport and a movie theater. He turned down the airport option because of its "substantial security." Holmes chose instead to attack the only movie theater (out of the seven near his apartment) that had posted signs banning permitted concealed handguns.[12]

Another sad example is the mass public shooting at a gay nightclub in Orlando, Florida in 2016. At least 50 people were killed and 53 others injured. As commented in the UK Daily Mail: "To make things worse, it took three hours from the time of the attack until the police entered the building." This is further evidence that law enforcement officers are unlikely to arrive in time to save lives.

As noted in a Crime Prevention Research Center (CPRC) report:

Attackers will generally shoot first at any uniformed guards or officers who are present (the Charlie Hebdo attack in Paris last year illustrates that point). Alternatively, they will move on to another place without uniformed officers. The first person shot at the Orlando attack, an off-duty officer who was guarding the nightclub, was shot at before Omar Mateen entered the nightclub. In this particular case, the police only arrived on the scene after the attack occurred. That illustrates another point: it is simply impossible for the police to protect all possible targets.

It is hard to ignore how these mass public shooters consciously pick targets where they know victims won't be able to defend themselves. And they do so for good reason given the number of mass public shootings that have been stopped by concealed handgun permit holders.[13]

Other points to consider:

- 81% of police support arming teachers and school administrators, if they are properly trained and vetted.[14] Utah and Ohio have been arming and training teachers. A survivor of the Columbine shooting who is now in the state legislature advocates arming teachers, which Colorado now allows.[15]

- After terrorists attacked a school in 1974, Israel mandated armed security in schools, provided weapons training to teachers and runs frequent active shooter drills. There have been only two school shootings since then, and both ended with teachers killing the terrorists. [16]

- The Marxist government in Venezuela confiscated guns from its population and now has a crime rate among the highest in the world, not to mention total control over its (starving) population. [17]

Defensive Use of Guns

Hardly ever discussed by proponents of more gun control is the defensive use of firearms. Two comprehensive studies found that there were between 1.5 and 2.5 million defensive uses of guns in the United States each year. [18-19] This means that firearms are used 80 times more often to protect the lives of citizens than to take them. The study authors explained:

Research has consistently indicated that victims who resist with a gun or other weapon are less likely than other victims to lose their property in robberies and in burglaries.

Victims who resist with guns are still substantially less likely to be injured than those who resist in other ways, and even slightly less likely to be hurt than those who do not resist at all.

In the case of rape, "victims who resisted with some kind of weapon were less likely to have the rape attempt completed against them." In fact, every year 200,000 women successfully use a gun to defend themselves against sexual abuse.

Commenting on gun control measures, the research authors warned that laws limiting the lawful use of guns, or discouraging their use could lead to less "saved lives, prevented injuries, thwarted rape attempts, [and] driven off burglars."

You may be asking, if there are so many defensive uses of guns by average citizens, why have we never heard about them? Good question! To make up this knowledge deficit, let me share just a few examples:

- Houston, Texas, March 27, 2018. A woman in her 50's was in her driveway when she was ambushed by three armed men wearing masks. They beat her, broke her jaw, and took her wallet. But when they tried to enter her home, she was able to shoot at them with her pistol, and they drove away.[20]

- Hemet, California, February 14, 2018. A gun was used by an elderly couple to repel a home invader who had a history of violent crimes in Southern California.[21]

- Stephen Willeford heroically intervened at the First Baptist Church in Sutherland Springs, Texas on November 5, 2017. The killer, Devin Kelley, was shooting parishioners when former NRA instructor Willeford, ran barefoot from his house across the street with an AR-15 semi-automatic rifle, forcing Kelley to stop his attack, presumably saving the lives of the 20 wounded and possibly many more.[22]

- Lyman, South Carolina, June 30, 2016. Two weeks after the Orlando massacre, 32-year-old Jody Ray Thompson opened fire on another nightclub. He was able to shoot three people before a concealed carry permit holder fired back and wounded Thompson in the leg.[23]

- Conyers, Georgia, May 31, 2015. A man killed two people at a liquor store and continued shooting at others until a permit holder ran inside and exchanged fire. The killer then fled the store. Rockdale County Sheriff Eric Levett commented, "In my opinion he saved other lives in that store." [24]

- Philadelphia, Pennsylvania, March 22, 2015. A 40-year-old man started shooting at people in a barber shop. A passer-by who heard the gunfire ran inside and shot the attacker. "The person who responded was a legal gun permit carrier. He responded and I guess he saved a lot of people in there," said Philadelphia Police Captain Frank Llewellyn. [25]

- Loganville, Georgia, January 4, 2013. A woman hiding in her attic with her 2 children shot an intruder multiple times before fleeing to safety. [26]

The finding of 2.5 million defensive uses of firearms per year in the U.S. suggests that there are more than 6,800 such events every day.

Concealed Carry Lowers Crime

Opponents of civilian gun use commonly fear that widespread "concealed carry" by average citizens will result in needless fatalities, envisioning what might go wrong with inexperienced users. But the truth is the vast majority of criminology studies have found that "shall-issue" concealed carry laws with minimal restrictions reduce crime. These studies show that violent crime falls after right-to-carry laws are adopted, with bigger drops the longer the right-to-carry laws have been in effect. [27]

The Crime Prevention Research Center reports that, while concealed carry permits tripled during the first seven years of Obama's presidency, the murder rate dropped 16% during that same period.[28]

Other facts to consider:

- Concealed carry holders are the safest segment of our society, as they commit crimes at a lower rate than police or the average member of the public.[29]

- The homicide rate in Florida fell 52% during the 15 years after a concealed carry law was enacted.[30]

- Kennesaw, Georgia required heads of households to own a firearm. Home invasions dropped by 89%. Ten years later the residential burglary rate was still 72% lower than it had been before the law was passed.[31]

Higher criminal home invasion rates are found in gun-control countries such as Great Britain[32] and Canada[33] than in the U.S. London's murder rate in February and March of 2018 surpassed New York City's as the British capital endured a dramatic surge in knife attacks.[34]

Predictably this has led to calls for "knife control" in the island nation. London Mayor Sadiq Khan announced a crackdown on knives in response to the rising levels of violence, saying "No excuses: there is never a reason to carry a knife." (Seriously?) "Anyone who does will be caught and they will feel the full force of the law." [35]

Given the "success" of gun control laws in the UK, I wouldn't hold my breath about the prospects for "knife control."

But lunacy is not confined to any one nation. Here in the U.S., California Governor Jerry Brown signed a law abolishing mandatory minimum sentences for criminals who use guns to commit crimes.[36] In other words, we need stricter laws for law-abiding citizens, but more leniency for criminals who deliberately use weapons for violent crimes? It makes no sense, of course, unless you're a leftist, pro-gun control politician.

9
Racist Origins of Gun Control Laws

A well regulated Militia, being necessary to the security of a free State, the right of the people to keep and bear Arms, shall not be infringed. Amendment II

The right to bear arms did not start with the 2nd Amendment. On April 19, 1775, before the United States even existed, local militia composed of well-armed colonists confronted and defeated British soldiers at Concord and Lexington. Many colonists lost their lives guarding rights they considered to be sacred.

English Common Law protected and even mandated the ownership of arms, which were understood to be "weapons for offense or armor for defense," not just tools for hunting. In the Assize of Arms of 1181, King Henry II proclaimed the obligation of all freemen of England to possess and bear arms in defense of the Kingdom and forbade a lord from "alienating (i.e. taking) them from his men." [1]

Of course this right was not given to slaves in America, and often not even to free blacks. Gun control laws were used to keep firearms out of the hands of African Americans from the earliest colonial days. In the New World, the earliest gun control laws were enacted during the 1500's in what is now

Mexico, to maintain Spanish colonial rule. "Similarly, in the sixteenth century the colony of New Spain, terrified of black slave revolts, prohibited all blacks, free and slave, from carrying arms." [2] In Louisiana, the French colonists outlawed weapons possession among blacks.[3]

The earliest American gun control laws were enacted just a few decades after the first English colonies were founded. In 1640, the very first gun control law ever enacted on these shores was passed in Virginia. It forbade blacks, even freemen, from owning guns.[4]

Firearms became readily available in the years after the Civil War and could be afforded by newly emancipated blacks and poor whites. In addition, blacks who had fought in the Civil War in the Union Army were allowed to keep their guns. White supremacists saw this as a threat and passed laws to disarm blacks, but laws alone were not enough. In order to carry out the disarming of blacks, the Ku Klux Klan was formed in 1866. They created gangs all over the South, travelling at night in large groups to terrorize black families and take their guns away. Black citizens without firearms couldn't fight back.[5]

Several states, including Tennessee and Arkansas, banned the sale of inexpensive handguns, the only ones that could be afforded by most black residents. Alabama and Texas imposed heavy taxes on handgun sales for the same reason.

In the early 1900's, other states such as Florida and South Carolina banned the carrying and ownership of handguns and repeating rifles, except for sheriffs and their "special deputies," meaning "company goons and the KKK."[6]

Such gun control laws were not limited to the South. The 1911

Sullivan Law required would-be gun owners in New York to obtain permits from the police. For disfavored groups, such as southern and eastern European immigrants, Catholics, Jews, and blacks, this was an impossibility.[7]

In the wake of the "ghetto riots of 1967 and 1968" Congress was so "panicked" that it passed the Gun Control Act of 1968 to:

shut off weapons access to blacks, and since they associated cheap guns with ghetto blacks and thought cheapness was peculiarly the characteristic of imported military surplus and the mail-order traffic, they decided to cut off these sources while leaving over-the-counter purchases open to the affluent.[8]

Defensive Use of Firearms by African-Americans

As pointed out by the American Civil Rights Union in its report, "The Truth about Gun Control, Racism and Genocide," there is a strong history of gun ownership by African Americans for self-defense:

In contrast to gun restrictions, the freedom to bear arms has repeatedly enabled black communities in America to defend themselves both before and after the Civil War. Private gun ownership proved instrumental in the defense of black communities in Northern cities during the 1800's. City militias suppressed white mobs attacking blacks in Providence (1831), New York (1834), Pittsburgh (1839), Boston (1843), and Philadelphia (1849).[9]

While blacks were typically excluded from official state militias, in several cities black communities raised their own militias. Black militias repelled white mob attacks on black neighborhoods in Philadelphia (1835) and Cincinnati (1841).[10]

In Memphis in 1891, a black militia group protected one hundred men who were fearful of being lynched for three nights. The night the militia went home, a white mob rushed the jail and lynched three of the black men.[11]

Following a series of Ku Klux Klan beatings and murders of civil rights activists in the early 1960s, armed blacks began to escort activists and guard their homes. In 1964 – 1965 the Deacons for Defense and Justice formed in Louisiana, Mississippi and Alabama to protect black people and civil rights activists.

It is well known that many urban areas with strict gun control laws have high rates of crime. As noted in the American Civil Rights Union report:

Washington, D.C., a majority black city formerly known as the murder capital of the U.S., has enjoyed plummeting crime rates following the Supreme Court's 2008 Heller decision, which found that the Second Amendment establishes an individual right to keep and bear arms exclusive of participation in a militia. Heller ruled unconstitutional the District of Columbia's extremely restrictive gun laws, which made it a felony to load a long gun in one's home, effectively banning the use of guns for self-defense.[12]

This ruling was denounced by former Supreme Court Justice John Paul Stevens in a March 27, 2018 Oped in the New York Times. He also called for repealing the Second Amendment.[13]

The ACRU report continues:

According to gun control expert Dr. John Lott, more than 72,000 adults owned long guns in D.C. when Heller was passed. Lott observes, "After the decision, almost a quarter of the adult population were suddenly able to legally use those guns for self-defense." Crime rates in the District dropped precipitously in the five years following the Heller decision. Crimes using guns dropped especially sharply. Robberies using guns dropped 11.3 percent;

assaults using guns dropped 30.9 percent; and the homicide rate fell an astonishing 52.3 percent.

Lott also notes that after the Supreme Court struck down Chicago's handgun restrictions in 2010, "murder and gun crime rates didn't rise after the bans were eliminated—they plummeted. They have fallen much more than the national crime rate."[14]

The report concludes:

Gun control has proven to be a useful tool for oppressing blacks politically and culturally in the United States, while at the same time rendering them vulnerable to criminals. Guns in the hands of law-abiding citizens, in contrast, have repeatedly protected ethnic minorities while also driving down crime rates in the most dangerous inner cities.

Gun Control and Nazi Germany

As pointed out by Stephen Halbrook in his book, *Gun Control in the Third Reich: Disarming the Jews and "Enemies of the State,"* our current gun-control debate is nothing new. The same arguments for and against were made in the 1920's in the chaotic times of the German Weimar Republic, which enacted gun registration of all firearms in 1931.

As described by Halbrook:

In 1933, the Nazis, led by Adolf Hitler, seized power and used the [gun registration] records to identify, disarm, and attack political opponents and Jews. Constitutional rights were suspended and mass searches for and seizures of guns and dissident publications ensued. Police revoked gun licenses of Social Democrats and others who were not "politically reliable." The Gestapo banned independent gun clubs and arrested their leaders. Gestapo counsel Werner Best issued a directive to the police forbidding issuance of firearm permits to Jews.

In 1938, German Jews were ordered to surrender all their weapons, and the police had the records on all who had registered them. Even those who gave up their weapons voluntarily were turned over to the Gestapo.

Hitler directed propaganda minister Josef Goebbels to orchestrate the Night of the Broken Glass. This massive operation, allegedly conducted as a search for weapons, entailed the ransacking of homes and businesses, and the arson of synagogues.

SS chief Heinrich Himmler decreed that 20 years be served in a concentration camp by any Jew possessing a firearm. Rusty revolvers and bayonets from the Great War were confiscated from Jewish veterans who had served with distinction. Twenty thousand Jewish men were thrown into concentration camps, and had to pay ransoms to get released.

When France fell to Nazi invasion in 1940, the New York Times reported that the French were deprived of rights such as free speech and firearm possession just as the Germans had been. Frenchmen who failed to surrender their firearms within 24 hours were subject to the death penalty.[15]

Most readers know what happened next to the disarmed Jews and "politically unreliable" during the reign of the Nazis. Well-meaning people in Weimar Germany, like today, advocated severe restrictions on gun ownership, such as bans of certain weapons and registration. They could not foresee how the road to a hellish future was being paved by what they believed were reasonable laws.

As pointed out in chapter 3, in the other major democides of the last century - in Islamist Turkey, the Soviet Union, Communist China, Communist Cambodia, Guatemala and Uganda, gun registration and confiscation preceded the mass killings in each and every one of these nations.

In their wisdom, the Founding Fathers of our country clearly stated in the Bill of Rights that every American citizen had inalienable rights, which come from God, including the right to bear arms. This wasn't for the purpose of hunting or sport shooting, but for self-defense. I believe what they believed: keeping and bearing arms is a God-given right that no man or worldly authority has the right to revoke. This is not just an American right. The ability to defend one's self and one's family is the human right of all people on the face of the earth.

10
Peace Police Peace Militia

"Peace Police Peace Militia" is the term my father used when describing how citizens will defend God's Kingdom. Peace Police Peace Militia is the way we take responsibility as citizens of the Kingdom of God to defend our precious God-given freedoms. It is manifesting the love of Christ on a local level, based on the age-old principle of ensuring peace through strength. Peace Police Peace Militia requires we move from the mindset of sheep to lion:

> *The wicked flee though no one pursues, but the righteous are as bold as a lion.* Proverbs 28:1

Being able to fight and defend the Kingdom is an expression of loving God and His people. Self-defense is not only a natural right of citizens; it is part of our moral responsibility.

I have always been passionate about evidence-based martial arts and have been a practitioner of Brazilian Jiu-Jitsu, Muay Thai boxing, Kali/Escrima, Samurai sword arts and firearms arts. This passion comes from my father who was a wrestler in his youth, an avid fisherman, hunter and promoter of martial arts and self-defense. Many do not know but my father created one of the first gun companies in South Korea manufacturing air guns, eventually producing the M1 Carbine and Vulcan Canon for the South Korean military.

Most comfortable outdoors in creation, he was the kind of person who could (and did) survive in any situation. He was a survivor of the infamous North Korean death camps. He was a survivor of false imprisonment and torture by Imperial Japan during the Occupation of Korea. Due to these horrific experiences he urged us to become people who were not only self-reliant, but who could also become guardians for others.

Central to my ministry is working with young people. I and other instructors in our congregation, teach combat mixed martial arts, which includes Brazilian Jiu Jitsu, Kali-Escrima, Muay Thai, and firearms training. I emphasize that the purpose of training is to be better equipped to love God and love your neighbor. If we love the Kingdom, we must be willing to fight for it. Some Christians might think that when the Kingdom comes, Christ will do everything, and we can just sit back and enjoy living in Heaven. Some envision a quasi-welfare state where everything is provided for you. But this is an unbiblical view of the Kingdom of God on Earth as Jesus explains our responsibilities in Matthew 19:28

> *Verily I say unto you, That ye which have followed me, in the regeneration when the Son of man shall sit in the throne of his glory, ye also shall sit upon twelve thrones, **judging** the twelve tribes of Israel.*

And in Matthew 24:

> *Who then is a faithful and wise servant, whom his lord hath made ruler over his household, to give them meat in due season? Blessed is that servant, whom his lord when he cometh shall find so doing. Verily I say unto you, That he shall make him **ruler** over all his goods.*

In I Corinthians 6:2 Paul writes,

Do ye not know that the saints shall judge the world?
and if the world shall be judged by you, are ye unworthy to
judge the smallest matters?

Being co-heirs with Christ means joining him in the ruling
of the Kingdom, by defending justice and expelling what
is evil and ungodly. God gave free will to His children;
He will not take it away, as we would then become robots
incapable of truly loving Him. Love requires the choice to
"love back." Even when Christ returns, because of free will,
there will always be the potential for evil. The hibernation
and reawakening of evil is described in Revelation 20:7-10.
The war of Gog and Magog takes place after the 1000 years
of Christ's reign on earth; the wicked gather together to
fight Christ. The co-heirs of Christ will need to be ready to
overcome the demonic forces.

Resistance Against Disarmament

To disarm the people...[i]s the most effectual way to enslave them.
–George Mason, *referencing advice given to the British Parliament*
by Pennsylvania governor Sir William Keith,

The Debates in the Several State Conventions on the Adoption of the
Federal Constitution, June 14, 1788

Before a standing army can rule, the people must be disarmed,
as they are in almost every country in Europe. The supreme
power in America cannot enforce unjust laws by the sword;
because the whole body of the people are armed, and
constitute a force superior to any band of regular troops.
–Noah Webster, *An Examination of the Leading Principles of the*
Federal Constitution, October 10, 1787

The fight for freedom began with the American colonists

resisting British attempts to disarm them. Relations between the colonists and the British deteriorated to the point where Americans denied the authority of royal rule and commenced creating totally autonomous militia.[1]

After the victory of the militia at the Lexington Green and Concord in 1775, the British retaliated by seizing and obliterating colonial firearms:

In Virginia, they seized twenty barrels of gunpowder from the public magazine in Williamsburg and removed the firing mechanisms in the guns, making them impossible to shoot.[2]

By 1777, it appeared that the colonists would most likely be defeated. Colonial Undersecretary William Knox, anxious to prevent any further uprisings, ordered:

The Militia Laws should be repealed and none suffered to be re-enacted, [and] the Arms of all the People should be taken away... nor should any Foundery or manufactuary of Arms, Gunpowder, or Warlike Stores, be ever suffered in America, nor should any Gunpowder, Lead, Arms or Ordnance be imported into it without Licence.[3]

It was the Americans' steadfast refusal to give up their weapons on both the individual and collective level that enabled them to ultimately be victorious.

The right to bear arms and form militias against tyrannical governments is part of our American DNA:

What, Sir, is the use of a militia? It is to prevent the establishment of a standing army, the bane of liberty .... Whenever Governments mean to invade the rights and liberties of the people, they always attempt to destroy the militia, in order to raise an army upon their ruins.

–Rep. Elbridge Gerry of Massachusetts,
1 Annals of Congress 750, August 17, 1789

Contrary to banning guns, the Militia Act of 1792 made gun ownership and militia membership a legal obligation rather than a voluntary option.[4]

The 2nd Amendment was written as a safeguard measure to protect American citizens from any future despots. It was meant to ensure that the people could take on the government if necessary, and that the citizenry would be able to use force as a last resort. The local militia was the substantial check against government power. The authors of the Constitution focused on the formation of militia, thus fulfilling the need previously met by a federal standing army. Most of the Founding Fathers viewed a standing army as the alter ego of a tyrannical government.

The Tenth Amendment was included in the Bill of Rights to clarify that the federal government had only those powers specifically granted by the Constitution:

The powers not delegated to the United States by the Constitution, nor prohibited by it to the States, are reserved to the States respectively, or to the people.

It was put in deliberately as a stand-alone reminder and warning to the forces which promote the cancerous growth of centralized power. Apparently, it was not enough.

Since the 10th Amendment was passed, the federal government has spent trillions of taxpayer dollars on items nowhere to be found in the Constitution. Where in the Constitution is power given to the executive branch to create federal agencies with tens of thousands of regulations? These regulations have the impact of law, but only Congress has the authority to create new laws. Who can stand up to this bloated bureaucracy, which shows little signs of shrinking?

The Bundy Ranch Standoff

We can get a glimpse of the kind of character needed to resist the federal government when it oversteps its bounds by looking at the Bundy family of southern Nevada.

Ammon Bundy and his brothers grew up on a family cattle ranch in Clark County, Nevada. The ranch was established by their great-great grandfather in 1877. For five generations, the Bundy family has run cattle along the Bunkerville mountain. Their homesteads were established before Las Vegas had even one person living in it. Nevada had only been a state for 13 years.

The Bundy forefathers built water troughs and holding tanks to supply water for cattle. Cliven Bundy, Ammon's father, expanded the water system, which greatly benefitted the desert wildlife, making hunting and camping much more possible. His hard work benefitted the state industry without costing the taxpayers one dime.

In 1890, the state of Nevada created a registry so that ranchers and others could deed their water and grazing rights. In this way, grazing rights were recorded and protected by the state of Nevada. These livestock and grazing rights were and are vested property - much like deeded rights to one's home. These rights can be sold, traded, or borrowed against. This means the government cannot take them without compensation. They are the lifeblood of the ranch, and are a valued heritage of the Bundy family.[5]

Enter the U.S. Fish and Wildlife Service, an agency of the Executive branch, which in 1989 listed the desert tortoise as an endangered species. A year later, its status was described as "threatened."[6]

Enter another agency of the Executive branch, the Bureau of Land Management (BLM). It designated hundreds of thousands of acres of federal land near Las Vegas for strict conservation efforts, largely to protect the desert tortoise. Among the conservation measures they required were to cease livestock grazing, and place strong restrictions on off-road vehicle use in the protected tortoise habitat.[7]

In the early 1990's, the BLM trespassed on the Bundy's property, demanding elimination of all ranching activity from the land. They told the Bundy's that the federal government did not recognize their grazing rights and that they must remove all their cattle.

The BLM established offices on the ranch, and posted signs which read:

"No more Moo by '92" and *"Cattle Free by '93!"*[8]

Cliven Bundy responded that they had no authority to take his family's heritage. In reality, these federal agencies had no legal constitutional authority to administer the land inside the state and therefore no jurisdiction to trespass or prosecute him.

In August 2014, BLM joined with 4 other federal agencies to enforce their unlawful trespassing to destroy the ranch. A massive military complex was set up on the range, armed with 200 hired guns. They tased Bundy family members, slammed them to the ground, and released their dogs on them. Cattle were brutally rounded up with helicopters and run to death. The newborn calves were left to thirst to death or be eaten by coyotes. The dead cattle were dumped into massive graves created by federal backhoes. The BLM also began destroying the water infrastructure constructed by the Bundy's over 100 years ago. They were told that if they resisted in any way, it would result in another Waco or Ruby Ridge.[9]

Before long, word spread and the Bundy's quickly gained support from activists, militias, constitutionalists and members of sovereign citizen movements. Supporters drove hundreds of miles across the country to support the beleaguered ranchers.

Veteran Brandon Rapolla from Oregon, was among them. "I'm a devout Christian," he said. "I prayed upon it very heavily. And within less than a 24-hour period, I got my gear ready and headed down there."[10]

While the feds had anticipated some resistance, they did not anticipate the hundreds of militia members who vastly outnumbered the federal agents on the scene.

The BLM finally had no alternative but to leave when faced with a peaceful but unyielding group of mostly armed men and women standing up for their God-given rights.

But the BLM was not done. They needed to teach the Bundy's a lesson. For if one ant thinks he can resist, then the whole colony may think they can resist. The next step was to jail the Bundy men, leaving their wives and children alone to maintain the ranch. As reported by CNN:

...according to court papers. Bundy and several others – including his sons, Ryan and Ammon Bundy – were indicted by a federal grand jury in 2016 after the showdown two years earlier against federal land managers on the open range where Bundy's cattle grazed and fed.[11]

In December 2017, US District Judge Gloria Navarro overturned the ruling by announcing a mistrial, and they were freed from prison.[12]

The Bundy's never threatened or harmed anyone during the long stand-off. The FBI, on the other hand, shot dead family friend Lavoy Finicum, as he had both hands raised after emerging from his car at a federal agency road block. He was shot in the back without a gun in his hand.[13]

In the state of Nevada, federal agencies have taken 5,072 water rights from the people, and deeded them to themselves alone. In his geographic region, Cliven Bundy is the last rancher out of 53.[14]

Despite the best intentions of our Founding Fathers, the Constitution has not been able to prevent the swelling of a federal government whose extortion methods have far exceeded the overreach of King George III on the American colonies.

The Bundy's have provided a great example of the character and courage needed to stand up to the abuses of federal power and for the liberties that were guaranteed in the Bill of Rights. Needless to say, they would not have been able to save their ranch without the 2nd Amendment.

Defenders of the Kingdom

In my opinion, the Bundy's represent the spirit of Peace Police Peace Militia. They are the kind of people who will defend God's Kingdom. The Kingdom will not be made up of servile Christians who have relinquished their freedoms to an insatiable centralized power, which is often unaccountable and eager to go far beyond its constitutional limits. The Bundy's and their supporters put their lives on the line to stand against the federal forces trying to increase their power by controlling local economies, arresting dissenters and even killing them.

Peace Police Peace Militia members are law-abiding, freedom-loving people, willing to defend what is rightly theirs. Peace Police take responsibility for maintaining safe communities. Peace Militia takes responsibility to defend the nation from enemies both foreign and domestic.

Government is meant to be the servant of humankind, not its ruler. It is the responsibility of Peace Police Peace Militia to ensure that government stays in its subservient position.

Participating in Peace Police Peace Militia means becoming a guardian for your community and nation. By following God's command, we are actualizing the most important commandments - to love God and love your neighbor.

11
The Choice

When people stop believing in God, they don't believe in nothing — they believe in anything. C.K. Chesterton

The legislators in Germany's Weimar Republic who passed gun registration of all firearms in 1931 may have had good intentions. Little did they know that within just two years the Nazis would take power and use those records to identify, disarm, and attack Jews and political opponents.

It's tempting to take our freedoms in America for granted. We've been blessed with freedom and prosperity undreamed of in many parts of the world. We imagine that the American people could never have their freedoms taken away without their consent. Well, guess what, in many ways, it has already happened.

In 2015, the U.S. Supreme Court ruled 5-4 that belief in natural marriage between one man and one woman was the expression of an irrational bias, and therefore unconstitutional. In that moment, those who believed in natural marriage, including tens of millions of committed Christians, were suddenly transformed into bigots in the eyes of the law. What was widely accepted and understood by most Americans just a few years earlier, was now a shameful sign of malicious prejudice.

If something as fundamental as marriage can suddenly be redefined by one Supreme Court vote, is there anything that cannot be thrown out with a "progressive" interpretation? The 1st Amendment? The 2nd Amendment? The 4th?

We have already seen calls for the repeal of the 2nd Amendment by a former Supreme Court justice and other public figures. We have seen leaders of one political party calling for gun bans and even confiscations.

In April 2018, one Chicago area suburb passed a ban on "assault weapons," which included semiautomatic pistols and semiautomatic rifles like the AR-15. If the 18,000 residents of Deerfield, Illinois are found carrying or possessing one of these firearms, they can be fined up to $1,000 per day. One resident gun owner declared to the city council: "You are bureaucrats that Thomas Jefferson warned us about!"[1]

We have seen many of the nation's media organizations give a high profile to youth who accuse 2nd Amendment supporters of having children's blood on their hands, even when it is evident in several cases that it was the government which repeatedly failed to prevent or halt mass shootings.

Due to this shifting of blame onto citizens who had nothing to do with these horrific acts, America is potentially one or two elections away from turning millions of law-abiding gun owners into criminals overnight.

We Are Watching What You Say

As discussed in chapter 5, daring to speak publicly about rapes and violence committed by immigrants in several European countries has led to "hate speech" convictions, not for those committing the criminal acts, but for the journalists or bloggers who honestly report about what is going on.

I witnessed first hand the limits placed on free speech in Europe when I attended an "Arms for Defense" conference last year in Lausanne, Switzerland. Several people with expertise on this topic declined to participate, explaining that they would be risking their careers to even speak about gun rights in a public forum.

Freedom of speech still exists in theory in the U.S., but increasingly not in practice. At the University of Michigan and other college campuses, speakers with conservative views have been shouted down and prevented from speaking by both threats and real acts of violence.[2] Meanwhile, campus security and police were ordered to stand down and allow these protesters to destroy private property and prevent invited guests from giving their presentations. Campus Leftists have also acted to revoke the charters of conservative student groups,[3] and to take legal action against conservatives for "thought crimes."[4]

Whether we want to admit it or not, the spirit of the self-righteous "brown shirts" is alive and well on many school campuses, with the same enabling moral cowardice from school administrators that allowed fascism to grow in Europe in the 1930's.

The problem is not just cancelled speakers. Despite a host of well-funded "diversity" programs, most of America's universities are not diverse at all in terms of the ideas and political affiliations of their professors. A 2016 study of faculty voter registration at 40 leading universities revealed that out of more than 7,000 professors, Democrats outnumbered

Republicans 12 to 1, making it highly unlikely that students will be exposed to many, if any, conservative viewpoints. Out of five departments analyzed, the least hostile field to conservative scholars was economics, where there were still 4.5 leftist professors to every conservative. History was by far the most conservative-hostile department, where leftists outnumbered conservatives by a 33:1 ratio.[5]

Our understanding of the past shapes our perception of what is valuable to our nation and what direction to take in the future. Due to this imbalance of viewpoints in our colleges, the rising popularity of socialism among millennials is predictable. The truth is, many students have never learned about socialism's problematic and even deadly history. Most have never heard about the enormous sacrifices needed to establish the freedoms they take for granted.

Ken Holmes, a distinguished fellow at the Heritage Foundation, expressed his concern that increasing intellectual homogeneity in academia does not bode well for the health of the American republic:

It's no longer about trying to teach people to think critically but about trying to indoctrinate them to a certain point of view.[6]

Students who have been taught to avoid ideas that make them feel uncomfortable could care less about protecting the right to free speech. But it is precisely this right which allows Americans to debate, compare and test ideas and find solutions. Without this right we are simply no longer a free country.

The problem is not just on college campuses. Youtube, Facebook and Twitter have aligned with leftwing groups, such as the Soros-funded Southern Poverty Law Center, to shut down broadcasts of conservative, Christian and pro-

2nd Amendment organizations as alleged "hate speech." Our Church's Youtube channels have had our live streaming capabilities stripped away for months—Youtube claiming our videos were "spam."

Youtube is the venue for two thirds of videos watched online by millennials in the U.S.[7] Its owner, Google, claims that it is an "open platform." But over 40 Prager University videos been placed on Youtube's "restricted" list making it difficult for many young people to access those videos or even be aware that they exist.

Check out the restricted videos, such as "Why Isn't Communism as Hated as Nazism?" and "Immigrants! Don't Vote for What you Fled"[8] for yourself and see if there's any reason to label them as dangerous. The answer is "no," unless you think that anything that challenges the Left's "multicultural" domination of speech is too harmful for young people to even consider.

The term "politically correct," was coined in the late 1920's by the Communist Party in the Soviet Union to describe how the views of party members needed to be aligned. Leftists on America's college campuses demand similar suppression of views and speech that does not follow their "party line."[9]

As mentioned earlier, our own Newfoundland Sanctuary Church Youtube channel was shut down on February 28, 2018. This was the day of our Book of Life Registration Blessing. Many church members and others around the world were thus prevented from watching the live broadcast. We are developing alternative venues so that such ideologically-driven disruptions will not happen again, but the biggest harm is to those who are being prevented, by Youtube, from even knowing about the existence of our broadcasts.

Leftist attacks on free speech are real and alarming, but at least there is an alternative media where conservative and biblically-based views can be expressed. My father, who invested hundreds of millions to establish *The Washington Times* newspaper as an alternative voice in the nation's capital, would be happy to see that the Leftist dominance of information distribution is being challenged.

It is disturbing to see Communist China praise western nations for following its practice of restricting free speech on the internet. China's state-run *Global Times* declared in an editorial, "Reining in social media appears to be the trend of governments"[10] which are suppressing alleged "fake news" and unauthorized opinions. This will only drive ideas underground, rather than allowing them to be tested and examined for their strengths and weaknesses. Of course, what authoritarian governments fear the most is a real competition of ideas.

We should let people from all ends of the political spectrum, not government or Youtube/Facebook/Twitter censors, figure out for themselves what is or is not, "fake news."

The Problem with "Multiculturalism"

Immigrants to America have practiced and celebrated their home country culture and language, even as they aspired to acclimate themselves to the predominant American culture. In the case of my own family, while my parents spoke mostly Korean, I remember my father staying up late at night to learn as much English as he could. He was proud that my siblings and I were fluent English speakers, but not happy with the liberal "progressive" influences that were taking over America.

The expectation that immigrants to the U.S. would assimilate began to change in the 1970's and 1980's with demands that government institutions actively work to affirm the unique identities of minorities. This approach is called "multiculturalism." It has been defined as "the support for the presence of several distinct cultural or ethnic groups within a society."[11] It has also been defined as:

...the view that cultures, races, and ethnicities, particularly those of minority groups, deserve special acknowledgement of their differences within a dominant political culture. That acknowledgement can take the forms of recognition of contributions to the cultural life of the political community as a whole, a demand for special protection under the law for certain cultural groups, or autonomous rights of governance for certain cultures.[12]

While seemingly good in theory, multiculturalism in practice stands as a challenge to the ideal of a constitutional republic, which is that all citizens should be treated equally under the law. The practice of multiculturalism by governments in many European countries has led to concentrations of large groups of unassimilated immigrants who feel alienated from the predominant culture. It has established areas where the values of freedom of speech and religion do not apply.

This approach has also led to governments criminalizing discussion and reporting about the problems arising from those policies. Those who express concerns about the risks of unassimilated immigrants are accused of being "hate-filled," "racist" or "Islamophobic." It takes courage to stand up against such accusations, but that has always been the case for those who dare to question the status quo.

To give another example, the Women's March was organized in the wake of Donald Trump's election, with the aim of "dismantling systems of oppression" and "building inclusive structures guided by self-determination, dignity, and respect."[13] Yet their commitment to "dignity and respect" for women was demonstrated in a bizarre way when they denounced the shutdown of the *Backpage* website. *Backpage* facilitates prostitution and the trafficking of women and girls,[14] but Women's March organizers say "sex workers rights are women's rights."[15]

Leftists are quick to claim that they are the ones who truly care about women's rights. If so, why do they support a venue that facilitates sex trafficking and prostitution? Why are they silent about Muslim men in many European countries who harass, rape, or assault women who wish to walk freely on the streets of their neighborhoods as they have done all of their lives?[16]

These Leftists appear to be unaware or indifferent to the history of abolitionist Christians who led anti-slavery movements in the United Kingdom, other European countries, and the United States in the 19th century. They seem not to realize that they would be among the first to be attacked, imprisoned or eliminated in an Islamized Europe. The massacre of journalists in the offices of the Charlie Hebdo satirical magazine in Paris is just one glimpse of what is likely to come.

Since multicultural policies do nothing to challenge Islamist extremism and instead perpetuate an environment where it can grow, why do Leftists continue to promote them? Could it be that their goal to destroy the Judeo-Christian foundation of the West is stronger than their supposed desire to preserve a society where women can walk on city streets, with clothing of their choice, without being harassed or raped?

As I learned from my father, the Left has always opposed

Peace through Strength. Had we followed their policies in the 1980's instead of President Reagan's, there might still be a Soviet Union exporting Communism throughout the world. My father always insisted that without the foundation of Biblically-based moral values, Western liberal democracies will not be able to stand against external and internal forces seeking their demise.

Which Choice Will We Make?

As I've repeatedly stated in this book, we are each responsible for our own self-defense. It is illusory to think that governments have the capacity to always protect us. When they try to do so, they often adopt tactics that only create more of a police state.

There is another approach that I believe will both protect freedom and provide safety, but it means taking responsibility instead of "outsourcing" all of our security needs to "professionals." If families are armed, criminals and potential tyrants will hesitate before trying to take advantage of or oppress them. The fact that all Swiss men were armed was an important reason why Hitler feared to invade that country. Up until now, satanic kings have been the ones who monopolized force. It is time for God's sons and daughters, who have no desire to oppress anyone, to defend their own families, communities and "kingdoms."

As followers of Christ, we are commanded to love God and love our neighbors as ourselves. Jesus clarified what this means when he said:

> *Greater love has no one than this: to lay down one's life for one's friends.* John 15:13

Aaron Feiss, the football coach at Stoneman Douglas high school demonstrated this kind of love when he shielded students with his own body. My question is this: Would you trust this kind of person to not just shield two students, but to have the means to save more lives? I would. Had Feiss been armed, he would have had the means to prevent many more lives from being taken.

The "professional" government-appointed deputy sheriff who had a weapon and was wearing body armor chose not to enter the school until the danger was gone. Jesus does not say "the greatest love is to call 911 and wait for someone else to do something." When good people have the ability to defend themselves, people with evil intent must re-evaluate their desires and their way of life.

Evil preys on weakness. We should seek to master the Way of the Rod of Iron, not to oppress others, but rather to protect others. The Rod of Iron is the greatest equalizer and force multiplier against actual corporate evil and tyranny. For materialists, this may be hard to understand because for them, a gun is just a violent weapon.

But, from a spiritual perspective, the person (not the gun) is the issue. Is the person holding the Rod of Iron, responsible, honorable, chivalrous and sacrificial like Christ? Is the person willing to lay his life down for his friends and to love God and love his neighbor? Is the Kingdom that is ruled by the Rod of Iron, honoring and protecting the freedoms and liberty God has given all His children?

The age where government centralizes and dominates all aspects of life is over. Families should no longer delegate control over their health, education and survival to bureaucracies whose agendas do not align with, or tolerate Godly values. As Christ's co-kings and queens, we must claim the sovereignty given to us by God, not to oppress others as satanic leaders do, but to empower and protect all of the peoples of this world.

God Bless, Godspeed and may **His** Kingdom come!

ENDNOTES

Chapter One

[1] Chronology of the shooting at the Stoneman Douglas High School in Parkland, FL based on reports from the Miami Herald. David Ovalle, Charles Rabin, David Smiley And Carli Teproff, "Disgraced Parkland deputy heard shots inside school building, told cops to stay away," Miami Herald, March 8, 2018.

[2] Eric Levenson and Joe Sterling, "These are the victims of the Florida school shooting," CNN, February 21, 2018.

[3] Liam Stack, "Clooney, Winfrey and Spielberg Donate Money for March against Gun Violence," New York Times, February 20, 2018.

[4] Carol Marbin Miller And Kyra Gurney, "Shooter revealed gory fantasies to his therapists years before the Parkland massacre," Miami Herald, March 9, 2018.

[5] Guy Benson, "More Signs: Parkland Killer Revealed 'Gory Fantasies,' Violent Impulses to Therapists For Years," Townhall.com, March 12, 2018.

[6] Paul Sperry, "Behind Cruz's Florida Rampage, Obama's School-Leniency Policy," RealClear Investigations, www.realclearinvestigations.com/articles/2018/02/28/obama_administration_school_discipline_policy_and_the_parkland_shooting.html

[7] Ryan Nicol, "Does Broward Schools' Program Coddle Troubled Students and Excuse Dangerous Behavior?" Sunshine State News, February 28, 2018.

[8] Tim Craig, Emma Brown, Sarah Larimer and Moriah Balingit, "Teachers say Florida suspect's problems started in middle school, and the system tried to help him," Washington Post, February 18, 2018.

[9] "School to Prison Pipeline," American Civil Liberties Union, https://www. aclu.org/issues/juvenile-justice/school-prison-pipeline

[10] Ryan Nicol, "Does Broward Schools' Program Coddle Troubled Students and Excuse Dangerous Behavior?" Sunshine State News, February 28, 2018.

Chapter Three

[1] Immanuel Kant, "What is Enlightenment?" 1784.

[2] Friedrich Nietzsche, *The Gay Science*, translated, with Commentary, by Walter Kaufmann, Vintage Books, 1974.

[3] Friedrich Nietzsche, *Twilight of the Idols AND The Anti-Christ,* Translated by R.J. Hollingdale, Introduction by Michael Tanner. Penguin Books. 1990.

[4] Friedrich Nietzsche (Author), R. Kevin Hill (Editor, Translator, Introduction), The Will to Power, Penguin Books, 2017.

[5] Rummel, Rudolph J., *Power kills: democracy as a method of nonviolence,* Transaction Publishers, New York, NY, 1997.

[6] Further discussion of these 7 examples of democide can be read in the article "Gun Control and Genocide," posted 5/14/2016. https://archive. org/stream/FiveCasesOfGenocideInTheTwentiethCentury19151995101/ Gun%20Control%20and%20Genocide%20-%20Mercyseat.net-16_djvu.txt

[7] Scott Manning, "Communist Body Count," December 4, 2006. https:// scottmanning.com/content/communist-body-count/

[8] New York Times Statement About 1932 Pulitzer Prize Awarded to Walter Duranty, https://www.nytco.com/new-york-times-statement-about-1932-pulitzer-prize-awarded-to-walter-duranty/

[9] Mary Anastasia O'Grady, "Why Venezuela Suffers: The regime enters phase two of its plan for a Pan-American revolution," Jan. 21, 2018, Wall Street Journal. https://www.wsj.com/articles/why-venezuela-suffers-1516566034

[10] Ibid.

[11] Persecution and Forgotten? A report of Christians Persecution and Oppression in the World 2015 – 2017. https://acnuk.org/country-profiles/

Chapter Four

[1] Dinesh D'Souza, The Big Lie: Exposing the Nazi Roots of the American Left, Regnery Publishing, 2017, p. 8.

[2] David Boaz, "What FDR had in common with the other charismatic collectivists of the 30s," Reason, October 2007. Reprinted by the Cato Institute, *https://www.cato.org/publications/commentary/hitler-mussolini-roosevelt.*

[3] David Boaz, "Hitler, Mussolini, Roosevelt: What FDR had in common with the other charismatic collectivists of the 30s," Reason, October, 2007.

[4] Wolfgang Schivelbusch, Three New Deals: reflections on Roosevelt's America, Mussolini's Italy, and Hitler's Germany, 1993-1939, Picador, New York, 2006.

[5] Ibid.

[6] Ibid.

[7] F. A. Hayek, The Road to SERFDOM, Fiftieth Anniversary Edition, University of Chicago Press, 1995.

[8] Jeremy Bauer-Wolf, "Column Stars a Culture War," Inside Higher Ed, December 1, 2017.

[9] List of ethnic groups in the United States by household income," https://en.wikipedia.org/wiki/List_of_ethnic_groups_in_the_United_States_by_household_income.

[10] Dinesh D'Souza, "The 'Anti-Fascist' Fascist," The Daily Caller, 7/31/2017. http://dailycaller.com/2017/07/31/the-anti-fascist-fascist/

[11] Dinesh D'Souza, The Big Lie: Exposing the Nazi Roots of the American Left, Regnery Publishing, 2017.

[12] Karl Zinsmeister, The "Anti-Hate" Group that Is a Hate Group," November 1, 2017. https://www.prageru.com/courses/political-science/anti-hate-group-hate-group

[13] Zinnmeister, op cit.

Chapter Five

[1] Magdy Samaan and Declan Walsh, "Egypt Declares State of Emergency, as Attacks Undercut Promise of Security," *New York Times,* April 9, 2017.

[2] Mustafa Akyol, "Why the Middle East's Christians are Under Attack," New York Times, May 26, 2017.

[3] Eliza Griswold, "Is This the End of Christianity in the Middle East?" New York Times, July 22, 2015.

[4] http://global100.adl.org/#map

[5] "Farrakhan Again Describes Hitler as a 'Very Great Man'" New York Times, July 17, 1984. See also, https://www.nytimes.com/1985/11/15/nyregion/editors-note-157088.html

[6] Thane Rosenbaum, "Palestinians are rewarding terrorists. The U.S. should stop enabling them," The Washington Post, April 28, 2017.

[7] Eli Lake, "The Palestinian Incentive Program for Killing Jews," Bloomberg News, July 1, 2016.

[8] Ibid.

[9] Evelyn Gordon, "Stop Subsidizing Terror Murder," Commentary, June 30, 2016.

[10] Lizzie Dearden, "Mohammed Abu Khdeir murder: Israeli man convicted of burning Palestinian teenager to death in revenge killing," Independent, April 19, 2016.

[11] Pew Research Center's 2013 survey report, "The World's Muslims: Religion, Politics and Society."   http://www.pewforum.org/2013/04/30/the-worlds-muslims-religion-politics-society-beliefs-about-sharia/

[12] David French, "Dispelling the 'Few Extremists' Myth – the Muslim World Is Overcome with Hate," National Review, December 7, 2015.

[13] BESA: A CODE OF HONOR- Muslim Albanians Who Rescued Jews During the Holocaust, http://www.yadvashem.org/yv/en/exhibitions/besa/index.asp

[14] Dan McLaughlin, "A Timeline Of Islamic Expansion In The Dark Ages,

https://www.redstate.com/dan_mclaughlin/2013/05/22/a-timeline-of-islamic-expansion-in-the-dark-ages/

[15] https://muslimreformmovement.org

[16] Hussein Aboubakr, "Where Are the Moderate Muslims?" https://youtu.be/Y9Enx4XxO1E

[17] "Banished at Brandeis: The university yanks an honorary degree for Ayaan Hirsi Ali," Wall Street Journal, April 9, 2014.

[18] Guy Milliére, "France: Toward Total Submission to Islam, Destruction of Free Speech," Gatestone Institute, March 19, 2018.

[19] Ingrid Carqvist and Lars Hedegaard, "Sweden: Rape Capital of the West, Gatestone Institute, Feb. 14, 2015. https://www.gatestoneinstitute.org/5195/sweden-rape

[20] Ibid.

[21] Melissa Eddy, "Reports of Attacks on Women in Germany Heighten Over Migrants," The New York Times, January 5, 2016.

[22] Soeren Kern, "Germany: Asylum for Cash Scandal," Gatestone Institute, May 22, 2018.

Chapter Six

[1] John P. Pratt, "The Prophetic Dream That Saved Martin Luther," July 14, 2010, Meridian Magazine,

 http://www.johnpratt.com/items/docs/lds/meridian/2010/luther.html..

[2] Martin Luther, Luther's Works, 33: Career of the Reformer III," (St. Louis: Concordia Publishing House, 1972) https://www.goodreads.com/work/quotes/4878257-luther-s-works-33-career-of-the-reformer-iii-luther-s-works..

[3] Nicholas P. Miller, "Luther, Locke, and Human Dignity," July/August 2017,

 http://libertymagazine.org/article/luther-locke-and-human-dignity

[4] John Adams, "From John Adams to James Warren, 22 April 1776," Founders Online. https://founders.archives.gov/documents/Adams/06-04-02-0052.

[5] John Adams, "From John Adams to Massachusetts Militia, 11 October 1798," Founders Online. https://founders.archives.gov/documents/Adams/06-04-02-0052.

[6] Edward Lynch, "Latin American American democracy is crumbling under corruption" The Hill, March 28, 2018.

http://thehill.com/opinion/international/380482-latin-american-democracy-is-crumbling-under-corruption

[7] Ibid.

[8] Hernando De Soto, The Other Path:the Economic Answer to Terrorism (New York: Basic Books, 1989).

[9] https://www.history.com/topics/black-history/madame-c-j-walker

[10] Tucker, marc. "Are We Just Fooling Ourselves? Is American Education a Colossal Failure? Education Week, April 10, 2015.

http://blogs.edweek.org/edweek/top_performers/2015/04/are_we_just_fooling_ourselves_is_american_education_a_colossal_failure.html

[11] Holmquist, Annie. "How a 1934 New York Graduation Exam Shows How Far Academic Standards Have Fallen." Intellectual Takeout, 10 May 2018,www.intellectualtakeout.org/article/how-1934-new-york-graduation-exam-shows-how-far-academic-standards-have-fallen.

[12] Thomas Jefferson, The Writings of Thomas Jefferson (ed. A.A. Lipscome and A.E.Bergh) Volume XV (Washington DC: The Thomas Jefferson Memorial Association 1905) 219-224

https://www.csun.edu/~hcfll004/jefflet.html.

[13] Constitutional Rights Foundation: Bill of Rights in Action, Fall 2010 (Volume 26, No. 1) http://www.crf-usa.org/bill-of-rights-in-action/bria-26-1-the-virginia-statute-for-religious-freedom.html

[14] *Thomas Jefferson, Notes on the State of Virginia, Query 17, 157—61*

http://press-pubs.uchicago.edu/founders/documents/amendI_religions40.
html

Chapter Seven

[1] Alexander Solzhenitsyn, *Godlessness: the First Step to the Gulag,*
http://www.pravoslavie.ru/47643.html

[2] Charles Carroll, *Letter to John McHenry.*
http://www.faithoffourfathers.net/carroll.html

[3] Peter Marshall and David Manuel, The Light and the Glory (Grand Rapids,
Michigan, Revel, 2009), 324.

[4] Marshall and Manuel, 324.

Chapter Eight

[1] "Emma Gonzalez's powerful March for Our Lives speech in full – video,
March 24, 2018, The Guardian, https://www.theguardian.com/us-news/
video/2018/mar/24/emma-gonzalezs-powerful-march-for-our-lives-speech-
in-full-video

[2] "Parkland Student Cameron Kasky: "Welcome to the Revolution," March
24, 2018, https://www.realclearpolitics.com/video/2018/03/24/parkland_
student_cameron_kasky_welcome_to_the_revolution.html.

[3] David Hogg: "Our Parents Don't Know How To Use A F*cking
Democracy, So We Have To," March 23, 2018,https://www.realclearpolitics.
com/video/2018/03/23/david_hogg_our_parents_dont_know_how_to_
use_a_fcking_democracy_so_we_have_to.html

[4] March for Our Lives, Washington, DC, March 14, 2018. https://www.
facebook.com/Mediamatters/videos/10155393898351167/

[5] Schumer to Walkout Students: This Time Gun Control Won't Fail
"Because We Have You," March 14, 2018,https://www.realclearpolitics.
com/video/2018/03/14/schumer_to_walkout_students_this_time_gun_
control_wont_fail_because_we_have_you.html

[6] "Parkland student and Second Amendment advocate asks why he wasn't invited to speak at weekend rally," March 25, 2018, https://www.theblaze.com/news/2018/03/25/parkland-student-and-second-amendment-advocate-asks-why-he-wasnt-invited-to-speak-at-weekend-rally?

[7] Eric Swalwell, "Ban assault weapons, buy them back, go after resisters: Ex-prosecutor in Congress," USA Today, May 3, 2018.

[8] Erica Thomas Full One-On-One Interview with Tucker Carlson, 3/26/2018. https://www.youtube.com/watch?v=89qeWpeqlVw

[9] "Fact-Checking Feinstein on the Assault Weapons Ban," ProPublica, September 24, 2014, https://www.propublica.org/article/fact-checking-feinstein-on-the-assault-weapons-ban. Also, see "2016 Crime in the United States, Expanded Homicide Data Table 4: Murder Victims by Weapon, 2012-2016" at FBI.gov

[10] David French, "Study: the Vast Majority of Gun Crime Isn't Committed by Lawful Gun Owners," National Review, August 12, 2016. https://www.nationalreview.com/corner/study-vast-majority-gun-crime-isnt-committed-lawful-gun-owners/

[11] More misleading information from Bloomberg's Everytown for Gun Safety on guns: "Analysis of Recent Mass Shootings," Showing how mass public shootings keep occurring in gun-free zones, Crime Prevention Research Center, September, 2014. https://crimeresearch.org/2014/09/more-misleading-information-from-bloombergs-everytown-for-gun-safety-on-guns-analysis-of-recent-mass-shootings/

[12] "Vince Vaughn explains the obvious: how mass killers pick out venues where their victims are sitting ducks," Crime Research Prevention Center, June 1, 2015. https://crimeresearch.org/2015/06/vince-vaughn-explains-the-obvious-how-mass-killers-pick-out-venues-where-their-victims-are-sitting-ducks/

[13] Mass Public Shooting in Florida occurred in ANOTHER gun-free zone: 49 dead in a shooting at an Orlando nightclub, Crime Prevention Research Center, June 12, 2016. https://crimeresearch.org/2016/06/mass-shooting-in-florida-occurred-in-another-gun-free-zone-as-many-as-20-people-died-in-a-shooting-at-an-orlando-nightclub/

[14] Ron Avery, "Police Gun Control Survey: Are legally-armed citizens the best solution to gun violence?" Police One Firearms Corner, April 8, 2013. https://www.policeone.com/gun-legislation-law-enforcement/articles/6186552-Police-Gun-Control-Survey-Are-legally-armed-citizens-the-best-solution-to-gun-violence/

[15] "US gun laws: Colorado to arm teachers in classrooms," BBC News, June 21, 2017, http://www.bbc.com/news/world-us-canada-40353408

[16] Tzvi Lev, "Israel proves the NRA's arguments," Arutz Sheva, February 21, 2018. http://www.israelnationalnews.com/Articles/Article.aspx/21714

[17] "Venezuela just crushed 2,000 guns in public, but the country is still awash in weaponry," Business Insider, August 18, 2016,

http://www.businessinsider.com/r-venezuela-crushes-2000-guns-in-public-plans-registry-of-bullets-2016-8

[18] Philip J. Cook and Jens Ludwig, "Guns in America: National Survey on Private Ownership and Use of Firearms," NIJ Research in Brief (May 1997); available at https://www.ncjrs.gov/app/publications/abstract.aspx?ID=165476

[19] Gary Kleck, Marc Gertz, Armed Resistance to Crime: The Prevalence and Nature of Self-Defense with a Gun, 86 J. Crim. L. & Criminology 150 (1995-1996).

[20] Lea Wilson, "Woman shoots at armed, masked men after attack outside southwest Houston home," March 27, 2018. https://www.click2houston.com/news/woman-shoots-at-armed-masked-men-after-attack-outside-southwest-houston-home

[21] Nicole Hayden, "Senior couple from Hemet shoots suspected home invader; suspect later arrested at hospital," The Desert Sun, Feb. 16, 2018. https://www.desertsun.com/story/news/crime_courts/2018/02/16/gun-protects-elderly-couple-violent-home-invader-hemet/346582002/

[22] "Man who opened fire on Texas church shooter hailed as 'good Samaritan," Associated Press, November 7, 2017.

[23] Jessica Chasmar, "Concealed carrier takes down shooter at South Carolina nightclub," *The Washington Times*, June 30, 2016.

[24] John R. Lott, Jr., "Good guys with guns saving lives," Crime Prevention Research Center, Nov, 12, 2017. http://crimepreventionresearchcenter.nationbuilder.com/good_guys_with_guns_saving_lives

[25] Ibid.

[26] Ibid.

[27] John R. Lott, Jr., "What a Balancing Test Will Show for Right-To-Carry Laws," Maryland Law Review, Vol. 71, 1205-1218.

[28] Lott, John R., Concealed Carry Permit Holders Across the United States: 2016 (July 26, 2016). Available at SSRN: https://ssrn.com/abstract=2814691or http://dx.doi.org/10.2139/ssrn.2814691

[29] Discussed in Gun Control Fact Sheet 2004 from the Gun Owners Foundation, https://www.gunowners.org/fs0404.htm

[30] Florida's murder rate was 11.4 per 100,000 in 1987, but only 5.5 in 2002. Compare Federal Bureau of Investigation, "Crime in the United States," Uniform Crime Reports, (1988): 7, 53; and FBI, (2003):19, 79.

[31] Gary Kleck, "Crime Control Through the Private Use of Armed Force," Social Problems 35 (February 1988):15. Chief Dwaine L. Wilson, City of Kennesaw Police Department, "Month to Month Statistics: 1991." (Residential burglary rates from 1981-1991 based on statistics for the months of March - October.)

[32] "Most Crime Worse in England Than US, Study Says," Reuters (October 11, 1998). See also Bureau of Justice Statistics, Crime and Justice in the United States and in England and Wales, 1981-96 (Oct. 1998).

[33] Gary A. Mauser, "The Failed Experiment: Gun Control and Public Safety in Canada, Australia, England and Wales," Public Policy Sources (The Fraser Institute, November 2003), no. 71:4. This study can be accessed at https://www.fraserinstitute.org/studies/failed-experiment-gun-control-and-public-safety-in-canada-australia-england-and-wales

[34] Andrew Gilligan, "London murder rate beats New York as stabbings surge," The Times, April 1, 2018. https://www.thetimes.co.uk/edition/news/london-murder-rate-beats-new-york-as-stabbings-surge-f59w0xqs0

[35] William Cummings, , "After murder rate passes NYC, London Mayor

Sadiq Khan calls for sharper knife control," USA TODAY, April 9, 2018.

[36] Larry Keane, "California Eases up on Gun Crimes, While Restricting Gun Rights," November 1, 2017. https://www.nssf.org/california-eases-up-on-gun-crimes-while-restricting-gun-rights/

Chapter Nine

[1] For more discussion about the historical background of the right, and duty, for the means to self-defense, see David T. Hardy, "Armed Citizens, Citizen Armies: Towards a Jurisprudence of the Second Amendment," *Harvard Journal of Law & Public Policy, 1986.*

[2] Michael C. Meyer and William L. Sherman, The Course of Mexican History, 4th ed., (New York, Oxford University Press: 1991), p. 216.

[3] "The Truth about Gun Control, Racism and Genocide," 2015. American Civil Rights Union, 3213 Duke St., #625, Alexandria, VA 22314.

[4] Ibid.

[5] Adam Winkler, "Is Gun Control Racist?," http://www.thedailybeast.com/articles/2011/10/09/adam-winkler-gun-fight-author-on-gun-control-s-racism.html

[6] William R. Tonso, "Gun Control: White Man's Law," Reason Magazine, December 1985, http://www.guncite.com/journals/gun_control_wtr8512.html

[7] For more discussion about discrimination in the application of gun laws, see J. Baxter Stegall, "The Curse of Ham: Disarmament through Discrimination - the Necessity of Applying Strict Scrutiny to Second Amendment Issues in Order to Prevent Racial Discrimination by States and Localities through Gun Control Laws." *Liberty University Law Review*, Volume 11, Issue 1, Article 10.

[8] Op cit., "The Truth about Gun Control, Racism and Genocide,"

[9] Ibid.

[10] Robert J. Cottrol and Raymond T. Diamond, The Second Amendment:

Toward an Afro-Americanist Reconsideration, http://www.guncite.com/journals/cd-recon.html#h5

[11] Ibid.

[12] Ibid.

[13] John Paul Stevens, "Repeal the Second Amendment," New York Times, March 27, 2018.

[14] Dr. John Lott, "Updating the changes in DC's crime rates following Heller," http://johnrlott.blogspot.com/2012/11/updating-changes-in-dcs-crime-rates.html

[15] Stephen Halbrook, "How the Nazis Used Gun Control," *National Review,* December 2, 2013, https://www.nationalreview.com/2013/12/how-nazis-used-gun-control-stephen-p-halbrook/

Chapter Ten

[1] T.J. Martinell, "How the British Gun Control Program Precipitated the American Revolution" *The Shooters Blog*, September 4, 2015.

https://blog.cheaperthandirt.com/british-gun-control-program-precipitated-american-revolution/

[2] Martinell.

[3] Ibid.

[4] http://www.constitution.org/mil/mil_act_1792.htm

[5] Ammon Bundy, "BUNDY: The True Story-Official"

https://www.youtube.com/watch?v=GhNmZ2lWc9U&t=17s

[6] https://www.washingtonpost.com/news/the-fix/wp/2014/04/15/everything-you-need-to-know-about-the-long-fight-between-cliven-bundy-and-the-federal-government/?utm_term=.e26fe501f2c1

[4] https://www.biologicaldiversity.org/news/press_releases/2014/desert-tortoise-03-25-2014.html

[8] Ammon Bundy, "BUNDY: The True Story-Official," https://www.youtube.

com/watch?v=GhNmZ2lWc9U

⁹ Ibid.

¹⁰https://www.pbs.org/wgbh/frontline/article/the-battle-over-bunkerville/

¹¹Cnn.com. https://www.cnn.com/2018/01/08/us/cliven-bundy-charges-dismissed/index.html

¹²https://www.usnews.com/news/top-news/articles/2017-12-20/mistrial-declared-in-case-against-nevada-rancher-cliven-bundy

¹³Ammon Bundy, "BUNDY: The True Story-Official"

https://www.youtube.com/watch?v=GhNmZ2lWc9U&t=17s

¹⁴Ammon Bundy, "BUNDY: The True Story-Official"

https://www.youtube.com/watch?v=GhNmZ2lWc9U&t=17s

Chapter Eleven

¹AJ Willingham, "An Illinois town just banned assault weapons. The penalty if you keep one? Up to $1,000 a day," CNN, April 5, 2018.https://www.cnn.com/2018/04/05/us/deerfield-illinois-assault-weapon-ban-trnd/index.html

² Stanley Kurtz, "Year of the Shout-Down: It Was Worse Than You Think," National Review, May 31, 2017.

³Anthony Gockowski, "UW students petition to shut down YAF, punish leaders," Campus Reform, December 16, 2016.

⁴ Cinnamon Stillwell, "When Speech Becomes a Crime," June 28, 2006, https://www.sfgate.com/politics/article/When-Speech-Becomes-a-Crime-2532414.php

⁵ Mitchell Langbert, Anthony Quain, and Daniel Klein, "Faculty Voter Registration in Economics, History, Journalism, Law and Psychology," ECON JOURNAL WATCH 13(3), September 2016: 422–451.

⁶ Bradford Richardson, "Liberal professors outnumber conservatives nearly 12 to 1, study finds, The Washington Times, October 6, 2016.

[7] http://www.insivia.com/27-video-stats-2017/

[8] https://www.prageru.com/playlists/restricted-youtube

[9] "A little history of 'politically correct.' The Soviets invented it and the university tolerates it," The Washington Times, November 15, 2015. https://www.washingtontimes.com/news/2015/nov/15/editorial-a-little-history-of-politically-correct/

[10] "Governments worldwide explore internet management," Global Times, April 1, 2018.

[11] https://en.oxforddictionaries.com/definition/multiculturalism

[12] https://www.britannica.com/topic/multiculturalism

[13] https://www.womensmarch.com/mission/

[14] https://www.commentarymagazine.com/politics-ideas/feminists-sex-trafficking-womens-march/

[15] https://twitter.com/womensmarch/status/982689439574085634

[16] Yves Mamou, "France: No-Go Zones Now in the Heart of Big Cities," Gatestone Institute, May 23, 2017, https://www.gatestoneinstitute.org/10404/france-no-go-zones

www.rodofironministries.com